More Welsh*lives*

Gone but not forgotten

Meic Stephens

First impression: 2018

© Copyright Meic Stephens and Y Lolfa Cyf., 2018

The contents of this book are subject to copyright, and may
not be reproduced by any means, mechanical or electronic,
without the prior, written consent of the publishers.

The publishers wish to acknowledge the support of
Cyngor Llyfrau Cymru

Cover design: Y Lolfa

ISBN: 978 1 78461 562 8

Published and printed in Wales
on paper from well-maintained forests by
Y Lolfa Cyf., Talybont, Ceredigion SY24 5HE
website www.ylolfa.com
e-mail ylolfa@ylolfa.com
tel 01970 832 304
fax 832 782

CONTENTS

More **W**elsh *lives*

Gone but not forgotten

Author's Note

THIS IS MY third collection of tributes to my fellow Welshmen and women, and to others closely connected to Wales, following on from the publication of the 72 obituaries in *Necrologies*, published by Seren in 2008, and the 75 obituaries published by Y Lolfa in *Welsh Lives*, in 2012.

The present volume includes 41 further obituaries. Thirty of them appeared in *The Independent* between 2012 and 2017, four were published in *The Telegraph* and one in *Barn*. I am grateful to those publications for permission to reprint them here. The remaining tributes appear here for the first time.

Just over a quarter of the tributes are to poets. Writers, academics and painters make a strong showing, alongside a mix of people from the fields of acting, broadcasting and film, the law, medicine, the police, as well as comedy and angling. Five people in the collection were born outside Wales – in the USA, Belgium, India and England – and went on to dedicate themselves to Wales and things Welsh.

I have followed the pattern of the previous book in this series by arranging the obituaries in alphabetical order, and recording the date and place of their original publication at the foot of each one where appropriate.

I have resisted the temptation to revise or update the tributes in any significant way. Except for the most minor embellishments, they are presented in the form in which they appeared in the original publications.

It was my privilege to have known personally all of the personalities whose lives are celebrated in this book, and to count many of them among my friends. It was my good fortune to have been familiar with their work, and to have been culturally enriched by their influence. I trust that those of you who read these tributes will recognize, as I do, the deep debt we owe to those who worked so tirelessly for the good of Wales. I hope that their example may inspire others to fulfill their own potential as they realise the importance of living life to the full and of using one's skills and talents for the benefit of others, and that they can, by doing so, enhance the cultural life of Wales and re-enforce its precious heritage.

It saddens me that circumstances have prevented me from preparing and including a tribute to my great friend Morgan Gwynfor (Gwyn) Griffiths, who died on 29 April this year. He deserves to be commemorated for his substantial contribution to literature in Wales, as a campaigner for social justice and peace and against apartheid, and for his work in fostering links with our Celtic cousins in Brittany. It was a joy to work with him on the preparation of our anthology of Welsh literature, *The Old Red Tongue*. Over a long period of intense collaboration and detailed discussion, we never had a cross word. As Gwyn quipped when he addressed the audience at the launch of the book in Cardiff, he '… took a lot of the credit for that'!

I am grateful to Eirian Jones and her colleagues at Y Lolfa for bringing this book to publication, and for all they do to support writing in Wales.

I take this opportunity to record my gratitude to my friend and former colleague, Peter Finch, for his advice and support over the years.

I also thank Russell Thomas, my friend and neighbour, for his help in preparing the proofs of this book, and for chuckling in all the right places as he did so.

Meic Stephens
Whitchurch, Cardiff
June 2018

ALISON BIELSKI

Poet who tried to express the essence of love

ALISON BIELSKI'S PREOCCUPATION as a poet was with Welsh myth and legend which she used to sometimes startling effect both on the printed page and in constructions that owed something to Concrete Poetry and the experiments of the European avant-garde. She was aware of the typographical shapes made by poems and of the gestalt qualities of words, so that her work was of interest to visual artists as well as the literary-minded.

She found in myth and legend a dynamic source of material, using its treatment of such basic emotions as love, jealousy and death as pegs on which to hang her own responses to the modern world. When characters from the Mabinogion, that great collection of medieval tales, appear in her poems they do so not as cardboard cut-outs but as real people with something to say about the world today.

But her favoured form was the love-poem. Often in love, and twice-married, she wrote lyrics in which she attempted to express the essence of love, often with gnomic precision and a delicate aesthetic touch reminiscent of the *hen benillion* – the anonymous folk-stanzas which were sung to harp accompaniment. These verses of hers have a pleasing simplicity and directness but they reveal almost nothing of the lover or the beloved, so scrupulous was she in distancing herself from the emotional experience described. They sparkle like exquisite jewels in much the same way as the *englyn* or the *haiku*, and simplicity is all, but they are hermetically sealed and do not repay scrutiny by the reader seeking biographical information.

Her prosody also strikes many readers as unfamiliar

and off-putting. 'I like a poem to have good bones,' she once commented. 'The shape on the page, together with the surrounding white space, allows breathing space for carefully chosen words.' To this end, she created her own system of versification which employs internal rhymes, half-rhymes and cadences imitative of speech-rhythms, rather than end-rhymes. All clutter is removed – punctuation is reduced to a minimum and there are no upper-case letters. These were not devices of her own making but she used them consistently and sometimes brilliantly to heighten the effects of immediacy which she always sought. 'I want my poems to sing,' she said, 'to surprise but never instruct.' Many do.

Her method changed little over the years. Although she won a number of minor prizes and exhibited her work in continental Europe, she was virtually ignored in England and regarded with caution and suspicion in her native Wales: her work was too 'modern', too 'experimental', too 'difficult' to command the respect of our more conservative critics and editors. Despite this neglect, she stuck to her last, convinced of her calling as a poet and determined to follow the writer's craft come what may. For many years her poems were published by a myriad of little presses in booklets that are now collectors' items. She made her debut with *Twentieth-Century Flood*, published by Howard Sergeant on the Outposts imprint in 1964, and this was followed by *Shapes and Colours*, published by the Triskel Press in Wales four years later.

Alison Prosser was born in Newport, Monmouthshire, in 1925. Her family, the Morris Prossers, had been in the district around Tintern Abbey since the eleventh century and her great-grandfather had driven the first mail-coach from Brecon to Bristol, thereby making postal history. She was acutely aware of the Border land of Gwent, where endless invasions from sea and land, and the clash of Welsh and English cultures, have gone to the making of the people and the landscape, and she made this turbulent history one of the themes of her poetry.

After leaving Newport High School at the age of 16, she had secretarial training before becoming private secretary to the press officer of the Bristol Aeroplane Company in 1945 and then working in her family's engineering firm. Her first marriage ended with her husband's death after two years. She then took a job as welfare secretary to the British Red Cross in Cardiff, remarried and settled down as 'a writer-housewife', finding time to write despite the strain of having to cope with an alcoholic husband and two growing children. Voracious reading made up in some measure for her lack of higher education.

Her first hard-backed book was *Across the Burning Sand* (1970) but, because it was difficult in those days to reproduce collages and the more advanced of her concrete poems, that book consists for the most part of poems in traditional forms, though they dispense with capital letters and conventional punctuation. It was followed by *The Lovetree* (1974) in the Triskel Poets series, after which she fell silent until her last, most prolific phase. Only a few small booklets such as *Flower Legends of Wales* (1974) and *Tales and Traditions of Tenby* (1981) appeared in her name, so that many thought she had given up poetry. A private woman who took pains to guard her personal life against enquiries from nosy parkers and the plain prurient, she found solace in playing the organ and harpsichord, and in baroque music and the game of chess.

But then a selection of her poems appeared as *That Crimson Flame* from the University of Salzburg in 1996, a volume that gave a new impression of Alison Bielski as a lyrical poet of some range and power, and the same press brought out *the green-eyed pool* in the year following. Her last books were *Sacramental Sonnets* (2003), a cycle of 52 poems written in 1982 which she considered her most sustained and memorable work, and *One of our Skylarks* (2011). The sequence is based on the year's cycle and reflects Church liturgy and the legends of Dyfed, land of the Mabinogion, where she lived for more than a decade, working in Tenby bookshops.

From 1969 to 1974 Alison Bielski was, with Sally Roberts Jones, honorary joint secretary of the English-language section of *Yr Academi Gymreig*, the national association of writers in Wales. Her administrative skills helped nurture the fledgling body until such time as it was taken under the wing of the Welsh Arts Council and then, in due course, made autonomous with its own office and personnel.

Alison Joy Prosser, poet: born Newport, Monmouthshire, 24 November 1925; married first 1948 Dennis Treverton-Jones (died 1950; one son); second 1956 Anthony Bielski (one daughter, marriage dissolved); died 9 July 2014.

The Independent (16 July 2014)

DUNCAN BUSH

Maverick poet who stood apart from his contemporaries

DUNCAN BUSH, WHO has died aged 71, came to prominence in the 1960s, a decade which saw a flowering of poetry in Wales partly in response to the resurgence of political nationalism and partly because *Poetry Wales* provided a major focus and platform for the work of young poets. Like fellow-Cardiffian Dannie Abse, Duncan Bush was no nationalist but he was keen for his poems to appear in the magazine and took full advantage of the new opportunities opening up for Welsh writers in English.

Even so, he stood apart from most of his contemporaries in that he gave his allegiance to no political party but chose to plough his own furrow. A left-winger nevertheless, he was more concerned with the miners' strike of 1984/85 than with the demonstrations of the Welsh Language Society and the drowning of Cwm Tryweryn to make a reservoir for Liverpool Corporation.

'In most of my poems,' he wrote, 'the happenstance of birth and nationality doesn't come up. It's not a thing I have on my mind much, and I certainly don't wear it like a burning shirt. However, like all Celts I've always been grateful for not being English. Then again, I'm glad to have English as the language I work in. It's the one I grew up speaking and reading, the one through which I discovered the world and I celebrate it without guilt.'

Born in Llandaff North, a working-class suburb of Cardiff, to Donald Bush, a bricklayer, and his wife Linda, née Richards, who was a grocery assistant, he grew up in a home filled with books and newspapers. He considered himself 'cosmopolitan by birthright' because their neighbours and

13

friends in the port city were from the four corners of the earth.

When the lad was six the family moved to a bungalow built by his father in leafier Whitchurch on the northern perimeter of the city where he had easy access to the woods of Castell Coch, the mock-medieval castle built by the Butes that stands above the valley of the Taff. War-comics and adventure stories provided his staple reading and American films his chief form of entertainment, facts he was to celebrate in some of his poems.

His first novel, *Glass Shot* (1991), has a first-person narrator who works in a garage. Stew Boyle, half-Irish and half-Maltese, is straight off the streets of New York in his attitudes and lifestyle. He dresses like a cowboy, drives a Thunderbird and loves violent American movies. It's 1984, the long hot summer of the miners' strike. A young woman he calls Rusty comes in to have a tyre changed. Stew is smitten and stalks her through the urban landscape of south Wales 'like an Apache in the Wild West'. The result is terrifying as the border between reality and fantasy blur in the psychopath's deranged mind.

He presents himself as a misogynist and rapist but has a wide range of literary references and his language is sometimes intensely poetic, which led some reviewers to see the author in him, but Bush always strenuously denied it. Others recognized a post-modern novel with a strong streak of fantasy, Boyle being unable to distinguish between his 'real life' and his fantasies, with tragic consequences. The reader is drawn inexorably into the world of Stew's obsession in this gripping novel.

Mercifully, the book stops short at portraying scenes of sex-and-violence and points to the young psychopath's impotence rather than his virility. Asked whether one reviewer who took an unkindly view made him want to bang his head against the wall, Bush replied, 'Not in the least. The only head that needs banging is the reviewer's.' He was anxious to point out that he shared none of Stew's sexual and political hang-ups and, quoting Dennis Potter, commented, 'It took me a long time to get inside Stew's head and what I found there I didn't like very much. But a writer sometimes has to write about his enemy.'

Unclubbable and determined to make his own way as a writer, he once wrote to a friend, 'The truest role of the writer seems to me that of the renegade, or maverick. This is not a question of wilful individualism, the self-cult of personality, but of a different form of responsibility, one that prefers the silence of self-determination to the mentality of the bandwagon. One cannot keep on writing about the heroism of the miners, real though I believe it to have been. The world, and the book, moves on.'

His first poems, written shortly after the death of his mother, were mostly to do with work, or the lack of it, and with the lives of people he knew as a young man. Some were published by the Welsh Arts Council in *Three Young Anglo-Welsh Poets* in 1974, which first brought him to public attention. One of the best-known is 'Pneumoconiosis':

Know me by my slow step,
the occasional little cough, involuntary
and delicate as a consumptive's,
and my lung full of budgerigars.

He had a wider purview than urban south Wales, however. His fascination with the European avant-garde and modern Russian literature took him along paths little explored by his Welsh contemporaries writing in English. He translated a number of major French and Italian poets such as Baudelaire, Pavese, Montale and Mallarmé and co-edited *The Amsterdam Review*, a bi-annual magazine devoted to European literature in English translation.

So convincing was his portrait of the Russian poet Victor Bal in *The Genre of Silence* (1988) and his persecution under

Stalin that many readers took it to be about a real writer, but in that they were mistaken. Intermingling historical fact with fiction, it is a collage of verse, reportage and Bal's own 'autobiography'.

Educated at Warwick University, where he took a first in English, Duke University in the United States, and Wadham College, Oxford, where he received his doctorate, Duncan Bush taught Creative Writing at Gwent College of Higher Education in Newport (now the University of Wales, Newport). He and his wife Annette Weaver, whom he married in 1981, lived in St Donats on the Glamorgan coast, where she taught English at Atlantic College. They moved to Luxembourg in 1990 to take up posts at the *École Européenne*, Duncan on a part-time basis; there he was pleased to be 'at the very heart of Europe'.

His later poems, published in *Masks* (1994) and *Midway* (1998), deal with a wide variety of subject-matter. The joys of gardening, the crisis in farming, vagrants, minor criminals, tango dancing, football fans, the war in Bosnia, the Mississippi, the Mediterranean and Chernobyl, all prompted him into verse. He used a variety of voices, too, including those of a hill farmer's widow, a garage mechanic, and most memorably in his long poem sequence 'Are there still wolves in Pennsylvania?' a mentally disturbed Vietnam war veteran and his wife.

In *The Flying Trapeze* (2012) there are several poems in elegant French, others reflecting his travels in Australia, Greece, Germany, France, and the United States, and a few that are political satires about politicians such as François Mitterrand, and the horrors of Sarajevo. His last novel, *Now All the Rage*, appeared in 2007.

Duncan Eric Bush, poet: born Cardiff, 6 April 1946; survived by his wife Annette, and by two sons, Joe and Lucas; died 18 August 2017.

The Daily Telegraph (30 January 2018)

BETTY CAMPBELL

The first black headteacher in Wales

BETTY CAMPBELL, WHO has died aged 82, was the first black headteacher in Wales and one of the first in the UK. She was also a community leader in her home district, the multi-racial docklands of Cardiff once known as Tiger Bay, where the National Assembly is now situated. She devoted her life to teaching the children of poor families and fostering the interests of the working class in the capital city and beyond.

She was born Rachel Elizabeth Johnson on 6 November 1934. Her father, Simon Johnson, a sailor from Jamaica, was killed in the Second World War, and her mother Honora (Nora) was a bookies' runner working the streets of Tiger Bay who, when betting became legal, opened a bookmaker's shop in the city. Her family, of course, was poor. But Betty's dream from an early age was to be a teacher, despite a warning from her headmistress that secondary education was out of the question for a girl of her background. The bright pupil left Lady Margaret's High School when she was 17 and expecting her first child. She married the child's father and put off her dream for the time being. But she never lost her ambition to become a teacher. In 1960, now the mother of three, she entered Cardiff College of Education where in due course she qualified.

Her first appointment was in Llanrhymni but she soon moved to Mount Stuart Secondary School in Butetown, and there she remained for the rest of her career. At first some of the parents, even those of African heritage, were suspicious of her but she quickly won the affection of generations of children, becoming a popular and influential member of the community.

The curriculum in Betty's school was unique in its day. Without permission from the governors, an emphasis was placed on the history of black people in Africa and the Caribbean, with special attention given to the evils of slavery and to the civil rights movement in America. I recall seeing pictures of Martin Luther King and Harriet Tubman on the classroom walls and hearing the children singing '*Nkosi Sikelel' iAfrika*', later one of South Africa's national anthems. The headmistress always gave Welsh a central place in the school's life and curriculum.

One of the most popular activities was Black People's History Month in which pupils learnt about the cultures of black people in various parts of the world. It was Betty's wish to improve the self-respect of her pupils by presenting more positive images of themselves.

As a councillor on Cardiff Council – she was first a Labour member and then an Independent – she was chosen to meet Nelson Mandela on the occasion of his receiving the Freedom of the City in 1998.

She was a member of the Race Relations Board from 1972 to 1976 and of a Home Office advisory panel. She served on the Board of Governors of BBC Wales from 1980 to 1984 and was made MBE for services to education and the community. In 2003 she was made an Honorary Fellow of UWIC (now Cardiff Metropolitan University).

Although her focus was on Cardiff Bay, Betty Campbell gained a reputation in England through her work for the Paul Hamlyn Foundation, in particular as the author of research papers which brought her to prominence as an authority on the education of ethnic minorities.

Independently minded, she was able to argue passionately and fluently for the rights of her community. At the same time she was a charming, gracious, warm-hearted woman who was loved by her own people. I remember walking with her once along Bute Street and noticing how children and adults alike all greeted her as Auntie Betty. The suggestion that she should be commemorated in the vicinity of the *Senedd*, in the heart of Tiger Bay, is entirely fitting.

Betty Campbell (née Johnson), teacher and councillor: born Cardiff, 1934; survived by her husband Rupert, four children and a number of grandchildren; died Cardiff, 13 October 2017.

Barn (December 2017/January 2018)

JOSEPH P. CLANCY

Distinguished translator of Welsh literature

JOSEPH P. CLANCY was an American with Irish and French grandparents who became a renowned translator of Welsh poetry and prose into English. He tackled all periods, from *The Gododdin*, written in Old Welsh in the sixth century, to contemporary writers such as Gwyn Thomas, Kate Roberts and Bobi Jones.

In 1985 he was awarded a prize by the St David's Society of New York, where he had been born on 8 March 1928, in recognition of his contribution to an understanding of Welsh culture in the United States. At the time he was Professor of English Literature and Theatre Arts at Marymount Manhattan College where he had taught since 1948.

He had discovered the existence of Welsh poetry while reading Gwyn Williams's book, *Introduction to Welsh Poetry*, in 1953, after which he turned from his interest in the classics – he had already translated Horace's *Odes and Epodes* – and decided to devote the rest of his life to interpreting the language and literature of Wales.

After spending several years acquiring a reading knowledge of literary Welsh, he paid his first visit to Wales in 1961 and, four years later, published *Medieval Welsh Lyrics*, which was immediately recognized as the best rendering of the medieval masters, notably Dafydd ap Gwilym and some of his contemporaries, that had ever been done. Even Welsh scholars, not the easiest to please when their literature is turned into 'the thin language', were impressed. For the first time, it seemed that Welsh had found a translator capable of conveying the complexities of its prosody and making it sound like poetry in its own right.

Clancy followed this triumph, after several more visits to Wales, with another highly accomplished book, *The Earliest Welsh Poetry*, in which he attempted the well-nigh impossible – to render in intelligible modern English the Old Welsh spoken in the northern parts of Britain in the sixth century. Again he succeeded, even turning out a complete English version of Aneirin's long epic poem *Y Gododdin*, which commemorates a British defeat at Catraeth (perhaps modern Catterick) about the year 590. For good measure he added English versions of some of the most difficult poems in the Welsh language – those attributed to Taliesin, the Llywarch Hen saga and the cycle of poems associated with Heledd, Princess of Powys, in the ninth or tenth century.

With his election to membership of the Welsh Academy in 1971, Clancy's reputation as a translator was firmly established, and he was to clinch it in 1982 with the publication of a third volume, *Twentieth Century Welsh Poems*, which included representative work by all the great names of modern Welsh literature, including T. Gwynn Jones, R. Williams Parry, Gwenallt Jones and Waldo Williams.

His energy as a translator was prodigious. Having tackled most of the major periods of Welsh poetry, he set about the prose. He translated the work of John Gwilym Jones, Gwenlyn Parry, Alun Llywelyn-Williams and Saunders Lewis; the last-named, a Roman Catholic like Clancy, is generally thought to be the most distinguished Welsh dramatist of the twentieth century.

But his most admired prose translation was *The World of Kate Roberts*, a selection of 35 short stories and two novellas which was brought out by the Temple University Press in Philadelphia in 1991. Kate Roberts, the most celebrated of Welsh prose-writers, took as her subject-matter the stoical lives of the quarrymen-crofters of north-west Wales and their fortitude in the face of disaster, war, disease and economic misfortune. Clancy caught the nuances of her rich Welsh style as no other translator had done.

Clancy's move to Aberystwyth in 1990 seemed like a homecoming, he told me. After the metropolitan sprawl of New York, he found the small town on Cardigan Bay a very congenial place to live, with a church, bookshops, libraries, pubs, arts centre, promenade and university all within walking distance from his new home.

A genial man, he had made many friends among writers and teachers living in the area and was now able to spend more time visiting other parts of Wales for the purposes of research. His knowledge of the Welsh language and its literature was immense, and he immersed himself in the literary affairs of the country, but curiously, although he would always encourage others to speak Welsh in his presence, for he delighted in hearing it used as a living language, he could not speak it.

His settling in Wales, with his wife Gerrie, a writer for children, coincided with a flowering of his own muse. He had already published *The Significance of Flesh*, in which the influence of traditional Welsh forms was seen in his preference for the *cywydd*, with its seven syllables to the line and the stress falling alternately on the final and penultimate syllable. Although it is not possible to reproduce its effects fully in English, for it relies on a complicated pattern of assonance and metre, Clancy had an uncanny knack of suggesting a Welsh inflection or turn of phrase that gives his verse a rich, individual tone that is rare nowadays, even among Welsh poets writing in English.

A second collection of poems, *Here and There*, followed in 1994, in which he explored his American identity and the ways it had been enriched by his experience of living in Wales. A third, *Ordinary Time*, appeared in 2000, in which he was revealed as a love-poet of great tenderness and passion.

The interface between translating and writing creatively was the subject of *Other Words*, a volume of Clancy's essays published by the University of Wales Press in 1999. This book also contains a comparative essay on the Welsh hymn-writer

Ann Griffiths and the American poet Emily Dickinson, and a memorable statement of his own *Ars Poetica*, entitled 'On Trying to be a Christian Poet'.

In thinking about the nature of translation and the role of translators, particularly in the context of a bilingual Wales, he concluded that, while it was all to the good if English translation can carry Welsh literature beyond its native community, that process is not essential but something added to its primary value.

'There is a danger of thinking,' he wrote, 'that the worth of a literature is to be measured by its being translated, its being known on a world scale, its being compared and judged as though writing were a kind of Olympic competition. If not a word of Welsh had been or would ever be translated into English or any other language, the literature would still have accomplished what literature is for, by giving pleasurable form and a meaningful voice to the experience of its own people.'

For his work as poet and translator Joe Clancy was awarded an honorary DLitt by the University of Wales in 1998. He leaves eight children, 14 grandchildren and seven great-grandchildren; one of his sons, Thomas, is Professor of Celtic at Glasgow University.

Joseph Patrick Clancy, poet and translator: born New York City, 8 March 1928; Professor of English Literature and Theatre Arts, Marymount Manhattan College, New York, 1948–90 and Emeritus; died Glasgow, 27 February 2017.

The Daily Telegraph (13 May 2017)

ANNE CLUYSENAAR

Poet and authority on the work of Henry Vaughan

'POETRY IS MY "country"', Anne Cluysenaar told an interviewer, 'it is where I live – but this is not an escape, it is an adventure, a moving out into what lies, mysteriously, all around me. Hence my interest in science, which is a form of exploration which I admire for its questions, its discoveries and its sense of wonder.'

That adventure was brought to a brutal end on 1 November 2014 when she was murdered at Little Wentwood, a smallholding near Usk, in the Gwent countryside, which she shared with her husband Walt Jackson. Her stepson, 48-year-old Timothy Jackson, was arrested and charged with her murder. The literary communities of Wales and Ireland were shocked by this dreadful news.

Anne's background was more varied than most. Born in 1936 in Brussels, the only child of artists John Cluysenaar and Sybil Fitzgerald Hewat, both of whom were of Belgian-Scottish descent, she was brought to Britain just before the outbreak of the Second World War. She was educated at Anglican boarding-schools in Scotland and England, and latterly in the west of Ireland, where she learned Irish, before taking a double first in French and English literature at Trinity College Dublin in 1957. She became an Irish citizen in 1961.

Having begun writing verse as a child, while at TCD she was awarded the Vice-Chancellor's Prize for Poetry and her first collection, *Nodes*, was published by Liam Miller at the Dolmen Press. She also edited the student magazine *Icarus*, published verse in the *Irish Times* and was included in Alan

Swallow's anthology *New Poets of Ireland* (1963). She also painted and some of her pictures appeared in an exhibition at the Musée Charlier in Brussels in which the work of five generations of her family was featured.

A distinguished academic career beckoned. She took a lectureship at Manchester University and founded the literary magazine *Continuum*. But she broke off teaching for a while in order to read to the partially-sighted critic Percy Lubbock in Italy and then to work at the Chester Beatty Library of Oriental Manuscripts in Dublin. She resumed her career in 1961 when she began lecturing in English and American Literature at TCD and then, after taking a Diploma in General Linguistics at Edinburgh University, went on to lecture at King's College, Aberdeen.

In 1965 she moved to the new University of Lancaster, where she taught General Linguistics, English and American Literature and Stylistics, and introduced one of the first Creative Writing courses at university level anywhere in Britain. Six years later she went to Huddersfield Polytechnic as senior lecturer in Linguistics and Literature, then took a lectureship at the University of Birmingham and began regularly to take writing workshops in schools and the wider community.

From 1976 to 1989 she was senior lecturer in Communication Studies and then principal lecturer in English and course leader in Creative Writing (described as 'writing skills') at Sheffield Polytechnic. At the same time she founded and was first director of the Verbal Arts Association, later amalgamated with the body that became the National Association of Writers in Education.

After retiring from full-time teaching in 1987, she moved to Wales with her husband Walt Jackson to live on a smallholding. Almost immediately she involved herself in the teaching of Creative Writing in south Wales. She helped to plan the MA in the Practice and Teaching of Creative Writing at the University of Wales, Cardiff, and taught on the undergraduate and MA writing courses for several years thereafter.

She drew inspiration from the literary landscape of wherever she settled. Living at Llantrisant in Gwent, she founded (with Angela Morton) the Usk Valley Vaughan Association, among the aims of which is to explore and celebrate the life and work of the poet and doctor Henry Vaughan and his twin brother, the priest and alchemist Thomas Vaughan. The association's journal *Scintilla*, now a substantial and well-regarded literary magazine, was launched in 1996; it publishes articles about the Vaughans, essays by practising poets, and verse exploring, in modern terms, themes significant to the brothers. She also edited the *Selected Writings* of Henry Vaughan.

Nor did she neglect her own writing. Among her main collections are *Double Helix* (1982) and *Timeslips* (1997), both published by Carcanet, and *Batu-Angas* (Seren, 2008). The last-named is a verse-sequence exploring the life and work of the great Llanbadoc-born naturalist Alfred Russel Wallace, whose theory of natural selection was developed at the same time as Darwin's. Her most recent collections are *Migrations* (2001), which includes a long poem based on the epic of Gilgamesh, *Water to Breathe* (2005), and *Touching Distances* (2013), a diary sequence or poet's calendar consisting of 75 poems for December 2000 to December 2012.

By virtue of her long residence in Wales and selfless commitment to the country's literary life, she was elected to a fellowship of the Welsh Academy and I felt able to include several of her poems under the title 'Vaughan Variations' in my capacious anthology *Poetry 1900–2000* (2007) in the Library of Wales series.

Anne Cluysenaar was a woman of keen intellect and deep spirituality. For long inclined to Quakerism, she joined the Society of Friends a few years ago, although her modesty prevented her from speaking publicly about her Christian beliefs. Only in her poetry can her preoccupation with numinous themes be detected. Poetry was indeed her 'country' and she undertook her 'adventure' with exemplary fortitude, never losing the sense of 'wonder' that makes her work so attractive and uplifting.

Anne Cluysenaar, poet and academic: born Brussels, 15 March 1936; married Walter Jackson; died Llantrisant, near Usk, Gwent, 1 November 2014.

The Independent (14 November 2014)

ANTHONY CONRAN

Acclaimed poet and translator of Welsh verse

FEW OF THOSE who have tackled the sheer rock-face of translating Welsh poetry into English have succeeded as well as Anthony Conran, whose *Penguin Book of Welsh Verse*, published in 1967, revealed to a wider readership not only the social background to Welsh poetry over the 1,400 years of its composition but something of the complexities which are its hallmark and, for Welsh speakers, the source of so much of its delight.

In a long introduction, he explained the traditional function of the Welsh poet as elegist and eulogist, the pillar and buttress of his society, a role which has made Welsh poetry, especially in its heyday during the Middle Ages but even in our own times, about as different from English poetry as the Chinese. Welsh readers applauded his understanding of the ancient prosody and English readers admired the masterly, readable versions which he was able to make of poems so obviously unfamiliar. The paperback took its place with Thomas Parry's *History of Welsh Literature* (1955) and *Oxford Book of Welsh Verse* (1962) among the major fruits of literary scholarship in post-war Wales. A revised edition appeared as *Welsh Verse* in 1986 and is still in print.

Tony Conran's achievement was all the more remarkable for two reasons. First, he was born with cerebral palsy, which made his speech difficult to understand unless one had grown accustomed to its tortuous delivery. This severe handicap, however, was wholly overcome by his powerful intellect, cheerful disposition and passionate devotion to what he saw as the art of poetry and the poet's function, which he expounded with a stamina and erudition that usually reduced any opposing view into stunned but respectful silence.

I first had a taste of his rigorous dialectic in 1961 while a postgraduate student at the University College of North Wales, Bangor, where from 1957 until his retirement in 1982 Tony was research fellow and tutor – and 'permanent bard of the place' – in the English Department under the legendary Professor John Danby. His book-strewn flat was a mecca for anyone living in or passing through north Wales who had literary ambitions and it was there, over a limitless supply of good coffee and among the exotic ferns he grew so attentively on every spare surface, that we hatched many a scheme which was later to enliven the Welsh literary scene. Under his aegis, Bangor became for us the veritable 'Athens of North Wales' which some have made it out to be.

Tony was primarily interested in Welsh writing in English, or Anglo-Welsh literature as he always preferred to call it, and in making it susceptible to the influence of writing in Welsh. His articles in *The Anglo-Welsh Review* during the late 1950s, mainly to do with the work of Dylan Thomas and R.S. Thomas but taking in the industrial, English-speaking south Wales of which he had little first-hand experience but always wrote about with typical panache, were the first stirrings of a critical re-assessment which served as a prerequisite to 'the second flowering' of Anglo-Welsh poetry in the decade following.

The second reason why Tony Conran was so notable as a translator was that, although his knowledge of Welsh poetry was profound, wide-ranging and infectious, he was never able to hold a conversation in the language. He was born at Kharagpur in Bengal in 1931, the only son of an engineer employed on the Indian railways. Brought back to Wales as an infant to be reared by his grandparents in Colwyn Bay, he attended the local grammar school and in 1950 entered the university college at nearby Bangor, where he took a First in English and Philosophy.

It was in Chelmsford ('in darkest England'), where he was briefly employed as a clerk in a factory, that he began reading Welsh poems and making his first tentative attempts at rendering them in English. He had already, as an undergraduate, discovered Welsh poetry in the translations of the distinguished scholar Gwyn Williams, up to then the best available. The turning point in his career came in 1954 when, in a competition for an elegy on the death of Dylan Thomas, the adjudicator, Louis MacNeice, awarded him first prize.

He came to public attention in Wales with the publication of his first book, *Formal Poems* (1960), which won one of the early prizes handed out, somewhat limply, by the Welsh Committee of the Arts Council in the days when that body made no proper provision for literature. The book included not only straight translations of the medieval masters such as Dafydd ap Gwilym but also poems of his own making which reflected the civilization in which they had flourished. I think, too, that what also held great appeal for Tony was the religious complexion of the poetry in which he was now immersed, for shortly after graduating he had been converted to Roman Catholicism, the faith which he was to practise for the rest of his life.

Tony Conran was a prolific poet who often wrote his poems as gifts for friends on the occasion of their weddings, birthdays, anniversaries, funerals, and so on. As a poet, he saw himself not as a loner exploring his own inner world but as a man, part of a community, with specific responsibilities to fulfil by means of his art. He was to publish another dozen books of poetry, including four volumes of his *Collected Poems*, as well as a bewildering array of pamphlets, many from his own Deiniol Press, and was still publishing his work until well into his sixties. A full bibliography is to be found in *Thirteen Ways of Looking at Tony Conran*, a Festschrift published by the Welsh Union of Writers in 1995 as part of a day-long festival celebrating his life and work.

Much of his writing is Modernist in technique and experimental and multi-faceted in form, yet firmly rooted in the Welsh tradition of praise and celebration. Perhaps his best-known poem is his 'Elegy for the Welsh Dead in the Falkland Islands, 1982', in which he managed to combine remembrance of the sixth-century Welsh (or British) defeat at Catraeth with the deaths of British (or Welsh) soldiers at Bluff Cove. Some of his later work, such as *Branwen* (1989), was written for performance, and the greater part of it has a left-wing, Welsh Nationalist stance. His most mature, and demanding, poems are to be found in *Blodeuwedd* (1988), *Castles* (1993), *All Hallows* (1995), *A Gwynedd Symphony* (1996), *Visions and Praying Mantids* (1997), and *Theatre of Flowers* (1998). His last book contained the long autobiographical poem *What Brought You Here So Late?* (2008).

As a critic of contemporary Anglo-Welsh literature, Tony argued against anglicization, provincialism and suburbanization, and in favour of an awareness of the more robust, socially conscious Welsh literary tradition. At the same time, he was not averse in his own work to borrowing from other cultures, including Kathakali dance, the music of Mozart, the symphonic qualities of Wordsworth's poetry, Chinese *shih*, Irish ballads and the theories of Cubism – in a rich mix which also reserved a place for *cynghanedd*, the *englyn* and the *cywydd* of the native poetry. Few poets have been able to draw on such a breathtaking range of ideas and forms. A selection of his most important critical writings was published as *The Cost of Strangeness* (1982) and *Frontiers in Anglo-Welsh Poetry* (1997). In 1997, the year in which his physical condition began seriously to deteriorate, he was awarded the honorary degree of DLitt by the University of Wales.

Tony's domestic life was happy and the source of many of his poems. Never short of female admirers (as a bachelor he claimed to find in some of them the muses in whom he only half-believed), he married his wife Lesley in 1977; she became his amanuensis and collaborator in the numerous readings and performances they put on together. A particular source of pleasure was that, like their mother, his two daughters, Maia and Alys, are fluent Welsh speakers.

Anthony Edward Marcell Conran, poet and translator of Welsh poetry: born Kharagpur, Bengal, India, 7 April 1931; Research Fellow and Tutor in the English Department at the University College of North Wales, Bangor, 1957–82; married Lesley Bowen 1977 (two daughters); died Bangor, Gwynedd, 14 January 2013.

The Independent (17 March 2013)

BRYAN MARTIN DAVIES

Poet of the anthracite valleys of post-industrial south-west Wales

BRYAN MARTIN DAVIES was the first poet writing in Welsh to make post-industrial south-west Wales the material of his poems. A generation before, poets such as Gwenallt Jones, Kitchener Davies and Rhydwen Williams had sung the coal valleys in their heyday and during the economic crises of the inter-war years, but it was Bryan Martin Davies who celebrated them in the last phase of their rundown in the 1960s and 1970s.

Born into a mining family in Brynaman, Carmarthenshire, in 1933, he had first-hand experience of the break-up of communities that followed the closing of the anthracite pits and the social blight that came in their wake. He was particularly concerned about the decay of the Aman Valley's rich cultural life in which chapel and workmen's institute had played such a key part. Although he was angry with the governments that had allowed this to happen, and his support for Plaid Cymru notwithstanding, there was nothing overtly propagandist in his poems and he seemed to see himself as a chronicler of inevitable decline and the celebrant of a way of life that was about to disappear for ever. He had, moreover, an aesthetic appreciation of the scarred industrial landscape which is rare among Welsh poets.

Bryan was educated at the Aman Valley Grammar School and the University College of Wales, Aberystwyth, where he took an Honours degree in Welsh in 1954. After graduation and an MA thesis on Gwenallt Jones, he did two years' military service which he always looked back on with wry amusement: it was, he once told me, the making of him as a writer because it gave him a steely capacity to observe the

33

folly of the officer class and the time to look into himself and discover who he really was. It also gave him a taste for cigarettes and beer and the male company in which he delighted for the rest of his life.

Although he took the Welsh-speaking communities of the Aman Valley as his main source of material, never moving very far emotionally from the scenes and people among whom he had grown up, he spent many years as a teacher in other parts of Wales: first in Ruabon, Denbighshire, and later as Head of the Welsh Department at the Yale Sixth Form College in Clwyd.

In north-east Wales he enjoyed friendships with many poets, notably Euros Bowen, a late but prolific representative of Symbolism in Welsh-language poetry, in whose company he often went gallivanting around the pubs of the old counties of Denbighshire and Flintshire. There never were two more dissimilar companions: Bowen, an Anglican priest, saw himself as a Sacramental poet, rather like R.S. Thomas in his later phase, and was given to exegesis on the finer points of his religious beliefs and poetic craft, while the younger man would usually have settled for some good conversation about rugby and a few pints.

Bryan first came to prominence as a poet at the National Eisteddfod held in Ammanford in 1970 when he won the Crown with a sequence of poems entitled *Darluniau ar Gynfas*, which became the title of his first collection published later in the same year; the book was dedicated to the people of the Aman Valley. The poems are a powerful evocation of the villages, pits, miners, chapels, farms and cinemas which the poet had known in his boyhood. His sense of the decaying industrial landscape existing cheek-by-jowl with the still vibrant rural tradition of the Carmarthenshire valleys is reminiscent of the young Auden.

His feat in winning the Crown was repeated in the year following: in *Golau Caeth* (1972) he included not only the winning sequence on that theme but also a number of elegant poems on subjects from Welsh mythology and others suggested by the work of the French Impressionists. Most of these poems are written in free verse (as distinct from verse in the traditional metres for which the Eisteddfod awards its Chair) and using verse-patterns that reflected the 'open field' approach to prosody that Davies favoured.

A wider horizon is to be seen in his next two collections, namely *Deuoliaethau* (1976) and *Lleoedd* (1984). In the second of these are to be found poems set in Poland and Switzerland in which he questions the bearded orthodoxies of those countries and holds up a mirror to what he understands about himself as a poet and man, often with a light sardonic touch.

In his last collection, *Pan Oedd y Nos yn Wenfflam* (1988), he addressed darker contemporary questions, including the miners' strike of 1984/85 and the spread of AIDS, as well as the exigencies of approaching old age. The most remarkable poem in the book is '*Ymson Trisco*', a long rhyming ballad spoken by an old pit-pony in which the poet manages to discuss, among many other things, the effects of Modernism and Post-Modernism on the literature of Wales and the state of literary criticism in Britain.

There was a tension in Bryan Martin Davies caused by his awareness of living in an anglicized corner of north-east Wales and yet earning his living by teaching Welsh and looking back in so many of his poems to his boyhood in the staunchly Welsh-speaking Aman Valley. One of his most chilling lines, '*Ynom mae y Clawdd*', is to the effect that Offa's Dyke runs through the psyche of every Welsh man and woman who feels the tug of England and the English language. For all his sympathy with those of his compatriots who write in 'the thin language', he knew on which side of the Dyke he belonged but was prepared to explore the complexities nonetheless.

Although he was twice crowned at the National Eisteddfod and was usually to be met strolling around the festival's field and attending the lively discussions in the literary pavilion,

Bryan played no official part in its affairs except as an adjudicator from time to time. But his public lecture on Watcyn Wyn (1844–1905) in 1980 was acclaimed as a perfect example of what is expected of speakers on such prestigious occasions: informative, scholarly, witty and moving in its *pietas* for a man who, like the speaker, was a native of Brynaman. Watkin Hezekiah Williams (the name by which he was known to the Inland Revenue) had kept an academy in Ammanford where young men were trained for the Congregationalist ministry. He was, for Davies, something of a mythological hero in his radicalism and commitment to education among the common people, and the poet researched his life and famous hymns with an uncommon zeal.

Bryan also wrote two more remarkable books that were admired by those able to read Welsh. The first was a Welsh translation, published in 1983, of the Prologue to the *Canterbury Tales*, which he put in hand after one of his daughters had complained that she found the Middle English of Chaucer's masterpiece rather difficult. He accomplished the task with an assured mastery of the rhythm and rhyming couplets of the original and keeping its vivid images and tropes.

The second was *Gardag* (1988), a fantasy novel 'for children of all ages', in which he succeeded, without a trace of anthropomorphism or sentimentality, in empathising with a pair of foxes living on the Black Mountain, in much the same way as Richard Adams did when writing about rabbits in *Watership Down*. Bryan's fascination with foxes, in which he detected some of the cunning and indomitable resilience of the Welsh people, is to be seen in his essay which appears in English translation in the anthology *Illuminations* (1998).

His last years were sad and lonely: cast down by the early death of his wife and suffering from cancer, he nevertheless wrote a number of fine, intricate poems in memory of

Gwenda, a selection of which were published in the magazine *Barddas* in 2000. His true stature as an important poet of twentieth-century Wales was confirmed when they appeared in his *Collected Poems* in 2003.

Bryan Martin Davies, poet: born Brynaman, Carmarthenshire, 8 April 1933; married Gwenda (died 1996; two daughters); died 19 August 2015.

The Independent (15 November 2015)

GWILYM PRYS DAVIES

Advocate of Welsh self-rule within the Labour Party

GWILYM PRYS DAVIES, as he was before he became a Labour peer in 1982, played an important behind-the-scenes part in the political life of Wales, notably as special adviser to John Morris, Secretary of State for Wales between 1974 and 1978, and thereafter as a thinker about constitutional matters prior to the establishment of the National Assembly in 1999. After his elevation to the peerage as Baron Prys-Davies of Llanegryn, he served as a front-bench opposition spokesman on Wales and Northern Ireland until 1995.

It was as an advocate of a greater measure of self-government for Wales that he made his most lasting contribution to Labour Party policy, pursuing this aim with dogged persistence even when it was highly unpopular in some quarters. Although he was never elected to a parliamentary seat, he was in close contact with Labour MPs in the pro-devolution camp, and never tired of arguing the case with those, mainly members for constituencies in urban south Wales, who were against it.

He had begun trying to influence Labour policy on Wales and Scotland in the early days of the Wilson administration by writing for Richard Crossman, later Secretary of State for Health and Social Security, a number of memoranda on the political situation in those two countries. Not much notice was taken of his paper *Reform of the Machinery of Government in Wales and Scotland* but in it he was able to develop the arguments he had long held and it went some way to clearing the ground for later consideration of the issue.

A fuller exposition of his views is to be found in his pamphlet, published in both Welsh and English as *Cyngor Canol i Gymru: A Central Welsh Council*, which was commissioned by the Welsh Council of Labour and published in 1963 by *Undeb Cymru Fydd* (The New Wales Union), an umbrella organization attempting to rally patriotic Welsh people in the interests of their country.

Davies had entered politics after war-service in the Royal Navy and while an undergraduate at the University College of Wales, Aberystwyth, where he read Law and was President of the Students' Union. He began as a member of the Welsh Republican Movement, a small band of young left-wingers, mostly ex-servicemen, who were hostile towards the Labour Party on account of its broken promises on self-government for Wales and impatient with Plaid Cymru for its lack of social and industrial policies and the pacifism of its leaders.

In a memoir published in 1997, the poet Harri Webb referred to Davies as 'the most fierce Republican of us all' and recalled the reverence with which his fellow-students invariably talked about him. It was Davies who wrote the Movement's constitution and provided an intellectual basis for the skirmishes it mounted, which consisted mainly of such provocative acts as burning the Union flag at street corners and heckling James Griffiths, the veteran Labour MP for Llanelli who was to become the first Secretary of State for Wales in 1964. At the only general election fought by the Republicans, at Ogmore in 1950, their candidate received a derisory 613 votes and Davies came to regard the Movement as an utter failure.

While still a student at Aberystwyth, Davies had contracted tuberculosis, in those days a killer disease, but recovered after treatment in a sanatorium which was paid for by a charity to which Thomas Jones CH, President of the university college and a Labour stalwart, had access. It was thought that this fact may have had something to do, after the disbanding of the Welsh Republicans in 1957, with Davies's joining the Labour Party while most of the others, notably Harri Webb and Cliff Bere, threw in their lot with Plaid Cymru. Of his decision Gwynfor Evans later wrote, 'The loss of Gwilym Prys Davies was a particularly heavy blow to us. He had in him the making of a national leader.'

Davies kept in touch with his erstwhile comrades, particularly Harri Webb who would not hear a word said against him despite their different party allegiances. The dialectic between the two, published in Webb's book *No Half-Way House* (1997), is one of the most intelligent discussions of the tension between Plaid Cymru and the Labour Party in Wales to have survived from the early 1960s, before the call for devolution began to gather pace.

The by-election called in the Carmarthen division for July 1966, after the death of Megan Lloyd George, was a watershed in Davies's career and proved to be a turning point in Welsh politics. The Plaid Cymru candidate was Gwynfor Evans and Gwilym Prys Davies, who had been the charismatic sitting MP's understudy, was chosen to represent Labour. In the event, Gwynfor Evans was elected by a majority of 2,436 votes, thus becoming the party's first member to sit in the House of Commons.

His defeat was a personal blow for Davies. A shy man, not given to furthering his own interests, genial in private but lacking the common touch and sometimes dauntingly prolix as a public speaker, he was not cut-out for the hustings and blamed the Carmarthen fiasco on the local Labour Party's failure to muster its vote in the mining parts of the constituency. Nor was he much good in argument on the doorstep. 'I couldn't see things in black and white,' he told a reporter from the *Western Mail*. 'I always saw them in various shades of grey.'

After much heart-searching as to whether he should seek nomination in some other constituency, Davies now turned his back on active politics and gave up hope of ever going to Westminster. He returned to his practice as a partner with Morgan, Bruce and Nicholas, a firm of solicitors with chambers in Pontypridd which specialized in representing the victims of industrial diseases and which he had joined in 1957; his home was in nearby Ton-teg.

His work as a solicitor in the valleys of south-east Wales had confirmed him in his Socialist convictions and he took immense pleasure in coming into contact with leaders of the workmen's institutes in their last phase and with the economically blighted communities they served. His firm was involved in the tribunal which was set up after the Aberfan disaster of 1966 and advised the National Union of Miners in the strike of 1984/85.

Perhaps as consolation for losing Carmarthen, and certainly in recognition of his intellectual ability, his capacity for hard work and his devotion to the public good, in 1968 Davies was appointed Chairman of the Welsh Hospital Board, a post in which he remained until 1974. He claimed that one of the reasons why he accepted the job was that his father, who started life as a farm labourer in Llanegryn in Meirionnydd, had had a leg amputated on the kitchen table by the village doctor, there being no facilities at the nearest hospital.

During his six years with the Welsh Hospital Board, Davies proved to be a new broom in what had been the traditional preserve of elderly men. Against a background of hospital closures and a damning report on the mistreatment of mentally ill patients at Cardiff's Ely Hospital which had detected on the part of staff 'an unduly casual attitude towards sudden death', he gave marching orders to about 30 of the old guard who had been running the management committees and brought in younger people to replace them. He also visited every hospital in Wales to ensure that reform was being carried out speedily, facing opprobrium in some places for delivering rockets where he thought they were needed.

Among other positions he held were membership of the Economic and Social Committee of the EEC (1978–82) and the British-Irish Inter-Parliamentary Body (1989–95), from 1989 the vice-presidency of Coleg Harlech, and from 1997 the presidency of the University of Wales, Swansea. He was also a member of the University of Wales committee for the teaching of Welsh and a governor of Ysgol Evan James, a Welsh-medium primary school in Pontypridd named after one of the composers of the Welsh national anthem.

When the functions of the Welsh Hospital Board were transferred to the Welsh Office in 1974, other appointments quickly followed, notably the part-time post of special adviser to John Morris, Secretary of State for Wales, who was an old friend from undergraduate days and one of the Welsh MPs most sympathetic to the principle of devolution. Among the matters on which Davies gave advice from behind the throne were the constitution, health, the Welsh language, the rural economy, education, leasehold reform, housing, unemployment and social exclusion.

It was another heavy blow for Davies when, on 1 March 1979, the Labour government's proposal for a limited measure of administrative devolution for Wales was defeated at referendum, for he had made substantial contributions to the evidence submitted to the Kilbrandon Commission on the Constitution.

But whereas John Morris made the famous comment, 'When you see an elephant on your doorstep, you know it is there,' Davies went on thinking about devolution and preparing for the next test of public opinion which, again at referendum in 1997, turned in favour of a National Assembly for Wales, much to his satisfaction. By then Prys-Davies (he changed his surname by deed poll in lieu of his patronymic) had taken his seat in the House of Lords, where he was able to do his bit in helping the Bill's passage through the upper chamber.

After his retirement from his practice in 1993, he returned to a subject which had long exercised him: the legal status of Welsh. A fluent speaker of the language who had been brought up in one of its heartlands, he was deeply attached to it, passed it on to his children and was proud that his father, William Davies, had written a history of the parish of Llanegryn, his native place. His own handbook, *Y Ffermwr a'r Gyfraith*, had been published in 1967.

The meticulous way in which he went about mounting a critique of the Welsh Language Act of 1967, which had proved wholly inadequate in that it provided only for 'equal status' between the two languages of Wales rather than 'legal status', is described in *Llafur y Blynyddoedd* (1991), an icily revealing insider's account of Labour politics in Wales during the second half of the twentieth century. There he also recounted how, on taking his seat in the House of Lords despite his misgivings as a former Welsh Republican, he was allowed to swear the oath in Welsh as well as in English, the first peer so to do.

Davies's work on drafting numerous papers on the legal status of the Welsh language and the creation of a fourth television channel broadcasting in Welsh paved the way for the establishment, albeit under a Conservative government, of S4C in 1982 and a new language act and statutory Welsh Language Board in 1993.

After the establishment of the National Assembly in 1999, Gwilym continued to bring his keen mind to the question of how its powers might be enhanced, writing many articles and memoranda in which he displayed a staunch commitment to the cause of Welsh self-government which he had advocated for more than 50 years.

Gwilym Prys Davies (Gwilym Prys Prys-Davies), solicitor: born Llanegryn, Meirionnydd, 8 December 1923; married 1951 Llinos Evans (three daughters); Chairman of the Welsh Hospital Board, 1968–74; Special Adviser to the Secretary of State for Wales,

1974–8; elevated to the peerage as Lord Prys-Davies of Llanegryn, 1982; Opposition Spokesman on Northern Ireland in the House of Lords, 1982–93; died Ton-teg, 28 March 2017.

JOHN DAVIES

Historian with an encyclopaedic knowledge of Wales and the Welsh

JOHN DAVIES WAS the pre-eminent Welsh historian of his generation. He wrote the magisterial *A History of Wales* as well as books on the growth of Cardiff and broadcasting in Wales. He was also much in demand as a pundit on radio and television: many in the media regarded him as the fount of all knowledge about things Welsh and he enjoyed his reputation as 'an encyclopaedia on two legs', taking part in countless programmes in his rich Welsh and patrician English.

His history of Wales was written for Allen Lane as *Hanes Cymru*, the first book ever published by Penguin in Welsh. It was commissioned by Peter Carson, Penguin's editor-in-chief, and was originally intended as a Pelican, but turned out to be three times the length stipulated in the contract. Even so, Carson was gracious enough to accept the typescript without cuts and published it as a hefty hardback of some 700 pages in 1990. The book won a Welsh Arts Council prize and quickly established itself as the best one-volume history of Wales on the market; the English-language edition appeared in 1993.

The book's appeal lay in its broad purview, fascinating detail and startling but always illuminating comparisons drawn from the author's wide reading and travels in Europe, both east and west. It begins with the Red Lady of Paviland, a skeleton dating from the Upper Palaeolithic Age – of a man it now transpires – which was discovered in a cave on Gower in 1823, and ends with the disastrous miners' strike of 1983/84 and just prior to the creation of the National Assembly. Its last sentence reads: 'This book was written in the faith and confidence that the nation in its fullness is yet to be.' Patriotic but never flinching from unpalatable truths, whether about his countrymen or their English rulers, John Davies wrote out of his deep and scholarly understanding of Welsh history but so attractively that he made fellow-historians seem drab and curmudgeonly in comparison. His *Hanes / History* is still the standard text for student and layman alike.

In a land with a dire shortage of surnames, and to distinguish him from a dozen others of the same name, Davies was generally known as John Bwlch-llan, after a village in Cardiganshire where his widowed mother was schoolmistress and where he had been brought up from the age of seven. But he had been born in Llwynypia in the Rhondda Fawr in 1938. He was immensely proud of his family's mining background and when he came to write his first book, *Cardiff and the Marquesses of Bute* (1981), it was natural for him to dedicate it 'in honour of my forefathers, William Davies and William Potter, Rhondda colliers, creators of Cardiff'. This was a timely and piquant reminder that the mineral wealth of the south Wales valleys, exported via the railways and docks developed by the Butes, had been responsible for the rapid transformation of Cardiff from a fishing hamlet into the largest coal-exporting port in the world.

His book about the Butes was based largely on research for a doctorate carried out at University College, Cardiff, and Trinity College, Cambridge. He taught in the History Department at University College, Swansea, from 1963 to 1973 and thereafter, until his retirement in 1990, in the Department of Welsh History at the University College of Wales, Aberystwyth, where he was warden of Neuadd Pantycelyn, the hall of residence for Welsh-speaking students. A highly sociable man who was able to stay up all night talking, something of a bon viveur and a consummate gossip, he broke the mould of the prim, chapel-going, teetotal Welsh academic with his bohemian appearance, atheism and hard drinking – he would consume a bottle of good wine with every meal and then take his students on a pub crawl – and was loved for it. It is said the university college attracted a number of students every year simply because they knew of his epicurean habits and the good times to be had at 'Panty'.

I met John Bwlch-llan in 1962 when he was the first joint secretary of *Cymdeithas yr Iaith Gymraeg*, the society for the promotion of the Welsh language which had been formed that year. He was assiduous in corresponding with official bodies such as county councils and thereby collecting data on which the society, when it turned militant about a year later, would base its campaigns. We drove to many parts of the country trying, not altogether forlornly, to persuade sub-post-offices to put up the sign *Swyddfa Bost* as well as its English equivalent and asking local authorities to use the Welsh forms of their names on letterheads, bills and road signs. When, in February 1963, society members sat down on Trefechan bridge in Aberystwyth in a bid to get bilingual summonses, John Bwlch-llan was nowhere to be seen, having no taste for confrontation and public disorder, and he played no active part in the law-breaking and prison sentences that followed over many years. We remained good friends, nevertheless, and in 1965 he was best man at my wedding.

His next major book was *Broadcasting and the BBC in Wales* (1994), commissioned by Geraint Talfan Davies as Controller Wales and published to great acclaim not only among media folk but by a wider public. 'Broadcasting,' the Annan Committee had been informed in 1975, 'plays a more important role in Wales than in any other part of the United Kingdom'. Davies set about defining contemporary Wales as an artefact produced by the BBC from the opening of Cardiff's first radio station in 1923 to the late 1990s when public service broadcasting faced new challenges such as the creation of S4C, the fourth channel broadcasting Welsh-language programmes made by BBC Cymru and others. But this was no dry, corporate history: the book abounds with anecdotes, pen portraits and juicy quotes from the Corporation's archives illustrating the tension between London and the 'national regions'. In particular, the author obviously relished the contribution made by *Cymdeithas yr Iaith* in concentrating BBC minds on the need for better provision of programmes in the Welsh language: it seemed as if policy was sometimes being thrashed out in the boardroom even as Society members were demonstrating in the foyer of Broadcasting House.

Two years later he published *The Making of Wales* (1996), in which he demonstrated, with typical wit and aplomb, that it was urban development which had created modern Wales and that industrialisation had saved the Welsh language by keeping the Welsh at home and allowing for the creation of such essential resources as newspapers and trades unions. The book was dedicated to his wife Janet, a native of Brynmawr in Blaenau Gwent, one of the cradles of the Industrial Revolution, who is a novelist and historian in her own right.

The bond between them survived Davies's announcement in a television interview broadcast by HTV in November 1998 that he was bisexual and that he was 'coming out' not only to give encouragement to Ron Davies, the former Secretary of State for Wales and architect of the devolution process, who had been involved in 'a moment of madness' on Clapham Common, but to provide solace to others like him in a Wales which John Davies perceived to be strongly homophobic. He spoke tearfully about having had to give advice to students at Pantycelyn who were terrified their homosexuality might be exposed, without being able to admit he shared their predicament. He also paid tribute to his wife who, on being told of his homosexuality, quoted the lines from Shakespeare's sonnet: 'Love is not love / Which alters when it alteration finds … O, no! it is an ever-fixèd mark, / That looks on tempests, and is never shaken.' The pair, and their four children, remained on the best of terms for the rest of his life.

John Davies, historian and broadcaster: born Llwynypia, Glamorgan, 25 April 1938; Lecturer in History at University

College, Swansea, 1963–73, and Senior Lecturer in Welsh History at the University College of Wales, Aberystwyth, 1973–90; first Warden of Neuadd Pantycelyn, 1973–90; married 1966 Janet Mackenzie (two sons, two daughters); died Cardiff, 16 February 2015.

The Independent (19 February 2015)

HEATHER DOHOLLAU

Poet born in Wales who wrote in her second language of French

IF IT IS rare for a poet to write in a language that is not her mother tongue, Heather Dohollau was that rarity: born and brought up in Wales with English as her first language, she wrote almost all her poems in French. Her work was admired by French writers such as Louis Guilloux, Yves Bonnefoy, Jean Grenier and Pierre Jean Jouve, with whom she enjoyed close friendships.

She lived in France for more than 50 years, most of the time at Saint-Brieuc on the northern coast of Brittany where the municipal library honoured her with an exhibition and colloquium in 1996, shortly after her 70th birthday. Her reputation as a poet and critic was recognized in 2000 when the French government made her *Officier de la Légion d'Honneur*. By then she had published a dozen books in French, though she remained almost unknown in the United Kingdom.

Heather Lloyd was born at Tynewydd, near Treherbert, almost at the top end of the Rhondda Fawr, a granddaughter on the distaff side of the general manager of the Llwyn-y-pia collieries who was a descendant of Thomas Charles of Bala, leader of the Welsh Methodists. Her father, by training a draughtsman, worked for the Patent Office and soon after her birth the family went to live in Penarth, a genteel seaside town near Cardiff. There she was educated at a private school and began learning French at the age of six.

When her father lost his job and had to move to London, where he became a civil servant with the Ministry of Aircraft Production, she found employment as a bookshop assistant in Cardiff, which she held until she joined the Women's

Land Army in 1942. After the war, having taken a course in nursing, she took it into her head that she would like to live in France; the stimulus was the death of her mother and seeing *Les Enfants du Paradis* in a London cinema, but she also recognized in herself a deep affinity with French life which was to stand her in good stead for the rest of her days.

She went to Paris, living on her own, attending classes at the École des Beaux-Arts (she was a talented art student) and exploring the streets of a city just recovering from the German occupation. It was not long before she met Yves Dohollau, the man whom she married in 1951 and with whom she went to live on the small island of Bréhat, off the coast of Brittany near Paimpol. Although life on Bréhat was difficult, there being no fresh water, she earned a livelihood by keeping a small art shop; she stayed for seven years and two of her seven children were born on the island. It was her time there, she once told me, that had cut her off from English, but she was also fond of paraphrasing Wittgenstein: 'Since the body tends to rise to the surface of the water, one should resist and try to swim to the bottom'; there was something in her that could not refuse a challenge and she prized her independence above all else.

Having separated from her husband, who is not mentioned in any of her poems, she settled in Saint-Brieuc, earning a living as a librarian in the town. The book-filled house in the rue Brizeux where she spent the rest of her life was the former home of Louis Guilloux, the Breton writer, author of *Le Sang noir* and other novels, who was among her first friends on the mainland; she was also encouraged by Pierre Jean Jouve, poet and novelist, with whom she remained on intimate terms until his death in 1976.

Although she had begun writing poems in English while on Bréhat, in 1967 she turned to her second language, and all her subsequent writing was done in it. At first, it was the difficulty of expressing herself in French that she found stimulating and, at the start, she confined herself to prose.

Among her highly esteemed critical works were a monograph on Rilke and a long essay on Victor Segalen, author of prose poems in the Chinese style, reprinted in *Les Cinq Jardins* ('The five gardens', 1974).

But the poems started to come in French soon afterwards. The first volume of her mature period was *La Venelle des Portes* ('The alley with the doors', 1981), published by Yves Prié at a small press known as Folle Avoine who printed all her subsequent books. She continued to publish her poems throughout the 1980s and 1990s. A sequence reflecting her time on Bréhat appeared as *dans l'île* ('on the island') in 1985 and was reissued three years later. Other books included *La Réponse* ('The reply', 1982), *Pages Aquarelles* ('Water-colour pages', 1989); and *La Terre Âgée* ('The old earth', 1996).

Critical acclaim came slowly but surely, thanks mainly to Michael Bishop, Professor of French Literature at Dalhousie University in Halifax, Nova Scotia, who did much to introduce her to an anglophone audience by writing about her in academic journals. He also included a generous selection of her work in *Contemporary French Women Poets: a bilingual anthology 1965–1995* (1995) and contributed a major article to the symposium *Lignes de Vie* ('Life lines'), the transactions of the colloquium held at Saint-Brieuc in 1996. The approval of Yves Bonnefoy, one of the most outstanding French poets of his generation who was attracted by Dohollau's hermetic quality, also enhanced her reputation in France, while she came to the attention of American readers in 2000 when a special double number of *Poetry Chicago* included a group of her poems in English translation by Hoyt Rogers.

Dohollau's poems are imbued with a sense of wonder and a serenity that are expressed in abstract, visionary and sometimes oracular images, largely unpunctuated and non-realistic in the manner of much modern French verse. Some critics compared her work with that of Max Jacob, which she admired.

The vital source of Dohollau's inspiration lay at the bottom of deep water and to get at it she had to make considerable effort in her adopted language. Because she could no longer rely on old linguistic habits, she was forced to clarify her ideas and feelings before exploring them in greater detail. She was fascinated by the problems of working inside that other language but still puzzled by the mystery of where poems come from: (translation)

Two languages stride together
To the threshold of the page
And the one that takes precedence
Is not your mother's
But rather yours, my daughter
For it is in you that we are
Almost genuine

Her poems are full of references to walls, windows, doors, thresholds, passages, alleys, gardens, paths, landmarks, boundaries, and the word 'transparency'. Although generally optimistic, at times even prayerful, they hold no metaphysical certainties and cannot be said to be mystical. A typical image involves holding one's breath and squeezing into a sort of initiatory passageway: 'In the intermediary state, the world is real.' If a dark note is occasionally struck in her poems it is because she found a fundamental contradiction between the earth's plenitude and a void, a lack of religious belief, in herself.

Heather Dohollau believed the poet's task is to ask the age-old questions about the experience of being alive: (translation)

What remains for me is the memory of places
Where I searched by asking questions
To say what is
And the answers so long in coming
Were what made up those moments
The water pouring from the cup of my hands

Heather Lloyd, French poet: born Tynewydd, Treherbert, Glamorgan, 22 January 1925; married 1951 Yves Dohollau (seven children, two daughters deceased); died Saint-Brieuc, Brittany, 30 April 2013.

The Independent (7 July 2013)

JOHN UZZELL EDWARDS

Painter inspired by Celtic symbols and folk-art

NEVER MUCH TAKEN up by the Academy, the painter John Uzzell Edwards claimed to have trained as an artist by avoiding art schools. He took what he could from the artists he admired and taught himself the rudiments of painting by copying scenes he had seen only on postcards and in books borrowed from the school library. He had a natural talent as a draughtsman and began by drawing rows of terraced houses, derelict buildings, dilapidated pits and abandoned chapels, of which there is no dearth in upland Glamorgan.

When I first met him, in 1962, I was living in Merthyr Tydfil and he was in Deri, a former mining village near Bargoed, just over the mountain, where he had been born. I had discovered he kept a work-room (studio was too grand a word for it) not far from where I lived. Our friendship was sealed after I bought for the then not inconsiderable sum of five guineas an ink-and-wash drawing of a pit-head meticulously observed and executed with a confidence that makes it one of the most striking images of the south Wales coalfield hanging on my walls to this day. It was John's first sale and he never let me forget I had been his first patron.

After leaving Bargoed Grammar School, he had a number of manual jobs before being made redundant in 1956; even the mine where his father had been employed, and where he too would have had to work, had been closed down. But the demise of the coal industry was for him a first opportunity to pursue his dream of becoming an artist which he had kept from his teachers and family alike; that was why he painted in the back-streets of Merthyr, where his mother wasn't likely to venture, and not Deri. With money he had saved, and still only 19, he took himself off to Paris and thence to Switzerland where he saw 'real' paintings for the first time.

The autodidact never missed a chance to educate himself thereafter. In 1966 a chance encounter with a holidaying professor on the beach at Tenby in Pembrokeshire, where he had built a small shelter for himself with the help of fishermen, led to his being awarded a Granada Arts Fellowship at York University. On the last day of his tenure there he met Mary Whitfield, the woman who was to become his wife. They had a son, Charlie, now better known as the graffiti artist and gallery-owner who goes by the name of Pure Evil, and a daughter, Esther. John and Mary made their last home in Plas Coedffaldau, a former mine-owner's mansion in the upper reaches of the Swansea Valley, which he used as a studio and exhibition space.

John's standing as a painter of repute was confirmed by his receiving a Leverhulme Trust European Research Award, which enabled him to spend a year in Rome. In 1986 he was Artist in Residence at the Glynn Vivian Gallery in Swansea and he put on one-man exhibitions at the Humphries Gallery in San Francisco (1999), Tenby Museum (2000), the Mall Gallery in London (2001), the National Museum and Galleries of Wales (2003), and the Museum of Modern Art in Machynlleth; he exhibited in three consecutive years at the Euro-Celtic exhibition in Lorient, Brittany. In 1996 he was commissioned by the Shakespeare Institute to paint any character from the plays and, ever the Welsh patriot, chose Owain Glyndŵr.

Uzzell Edwards, after his initial fascination with the industrial landscape of south Wales, produced work which had to do with what he called 'pure painting', not picture making, and was driven by an exploration of Celtic forms and patterns such as he had seen in 1988 while travelling in Europe. He was also inspired by Celtic crosses, medieval tiles and panelling, Pictish knotwork, illuminated manuscripts and church wood-carvings. He was particularly drawn to the eighth-century St Teilo's Gospels which, as he often pointed out, had been made in Wales at roughly the same time as the Lindisfarne Gospels and before the Book of Kells.

More recently he made large mixed-media canvases inspired by, but not slavishly imitating, the patchwork patterns of bed-quilts, the making of which is something of a folk-art in Wales. These works have non-figurative outlines and vigorous textures created by layers of oil paint, applied with brush and palette knife. The exhibition of these huge paintings at the National Waterfront Museum in Swansea in 2011 and as part of a retrospective at St David's Hall in Cardiff in 2013 met with wide acclaim.

John was obsessive about his painting and if there was work in progress, as there usually was, would speak about it unprompted and at great length. A gentle man, he had a slight speech impediment which, I think, was the reason why he hadn't done well at school but which kindled in him a burning desire to express himself as a painter. It endeared him to his many friends and turned out to be the making of him as an artist.

John Uzzell Edwards, painter: born Deri, Glamorgan, 10 October 1934; married Mary Whitfield (one son, one daughter); died 5 March 2014.

The Independent (3 April 2014)

MARI ELLIS

Writer and historian of the Anglican Church in Wales

MARI ELLIS LED a busy life as the wife of T.I. Ellis, the son of Thomas Edward Ellis, the Liberal MP for Meirionnydd whose premature death in 1899 robbed his country of an influential advocate of Home Rule and canonized him as the lost leader of Victorian Wales. T.E. Ellis, who was appointed chief whip in Gladstone's government in 1894, is commemorated by a large bronze statue in the High Street of Bala, his native place, and by another in the quadrangle of the Old College at Aberystwyth, of which he was a staunch champion. Mari Ellis was once amused to overhear a neighbour say she had 'married the statue's son'.

Thomas Iorwerth Ellis, born posthumously in the year of his father's death, carried on his work as the indefatigable secretary of *Undeb Cymru Fydd*, a non-political organization known in English as the New Wales Union, which brought together many prominent Welsh people and, in the 1940s, lobbied the British government on behalf of Wales in such fields as broadcasting, land acquisition for military purposes, the Welsh language and the increasing demand for administrative devolution from Whitehall to Cardiff.

He was the very epitome of establishmentarian Wales, serving on innumerable committees to do with such bodies as the University of Wales, the National Library and the Church in Wales, and coming to the attention of a wider world as a member of the team representing Wales in the popular BBC programme *Round Britain Quiz* for some 20 years.

In all this multifarious activity T.I. Ellis had the practical and dedicated support of his wife Mari who worked alongside him in a voluntary capacity as secretary, amanuensis and researcher for his books, memoranda and journalism. She also encouraged him in his conversion to the Anglican rite, for he had been a member of the Presbyterian Church of Wales, that is to say the Calvinistic Methodists, before their marriage.

Between 1953 and 1959 T.I. Ellis published five volumes in the *Crwydro Cymru* series of travel books exploring the counties of Wales, their topography and cultural life, several of which are masterpieces of the genre, and he made a further excursion to London in 1970. In each of these books Mari Ellis is thanked for her companionship 'along paths old and new' and it was she who finished the London volume after her husband's death and saw it through the press in the year following.

Mary Headley was born in 1913 at Dylife, a lead-mining village high in the Pumlumon range between Machynlleth and Llanidloes in Montgomeryshire, where her father was an Anglican vicar. Unusually for the time and her father's station in life, she was brought up Welsh-speaking and never wavered in her commitment to the language in everything she did.

After attending the John Bright Grammar School in Llandudno, she read Welsh at the University College of North Wales, Bangor, graduating BA in 1936 and MA two years later, and then trained as a librarian. She worked in public libraries in Colwyn Bay and Kingston-on-Thames until her appointment to the staff of the National Library of Wales in 1944. Five years later she married T.I. Ellis, who until his appointment as secretary of *Undeb Cymru Fydd* in 1941 had been a lecturer in Classics at the University College of Wales, Aberystwyth.

A devout Churchwoman, whose membership of the Anglican communion had survived the bruising Disestablishment of the Church in Wales in 1920, Mari Ellis was one of its most distinguished lay women. She was regular in her attendance at Eglwys Santes Fair (St Mary's), the

Welsh Anglican church in Aberystwyth. A prolific contributor to the periodical press, she contributed a women's column to *Y Llan*, the magazine of the Church in Wales, and wrote (with her daughter) a lively survey of the parish churches of Wales in which her knowledge of saints, architecture, hymns, graveyards and incumbents was attractively displayed for the benefit of visitors. She also edited *Yr Angor*, the community newspaper for Welsh-speakers in Aberystwyth.

Her principal field of research was the group of Anglican churchmen known as *Yr Hen Bersoniaid Llengar*, who fostered Welsh culture between 1818 and 1858, often in the face of stern disapproval from their anti-Welsh superiors within the Established Church. It was they who kept Welsh scholarship alive until the advent of the new learning emanating from the Celtic Department at Oxford University and the University of Wales; they also revived the Eisteddfod as a national festival in which the common people could participate. Associated with the group were a number of lay women such as Lady Llanover (inventor of the Welsh traditional dress) and Charlotte Guest (translator of the Mabinogion), who held a special attraction for Mari Ellis because, she once told me, they were less backward-looking than their male counterparts.

She wrote so extensively about these patriotic people, in articles both popular and scholarly, in Welsh and English, that when she came to assemble them for publication she found they amounted to some 200,000 words and that no publisher would agree to publish them without massive subsidy or without making cuts which she would not countenance. The articles remain unpublished, a fact she did not conceal when, on the occasion of her 90th birthday in July 2003, many of her friends gathered in Aberystwyth to pay tribute to her.

Her other keen interest was in the emancipation of women. Unlike her husband, who never revealed his political opinions, she was prepared to wear her colours on her sleeve (especially after his death in 1970) and made no secret of the fact that, as a feminist *avant la lettre*, she was most comfortable in the ranks of Plaid Cymru, which she had joined as a young woman. Her advocacy of women's rights runs like a thread through her three novels and collections of essays, many of which first appeared in the women's section of *Y Cymro*. She joined *Merched y Wawr*, the Welsh equivalent of the Women's Institute, soon after its formation in 1967.

Only once did she complain publicly about the frustrations of being a housewife and mother: in a diary written in 1954 she wrote (trans.), 'Oh, if only I had two pairs of hands and two heads! One for writing and the other for knitting, one for thinking about letters and the other for spinning stories and articles. But what can I do – with a head like a turnip and one feeble pair of hands!'

A genial woman, homely in appearance but with a formidable intellect and scintillating in her conversation, she was often to be found in the stacks of the National Library beavering away amid the manuscripts and periodicals from which she unearthed the primary material for her articles and books. Whenever we met we talked (in an obligatory whisper) about W.J. Rees, vicar of Cascob in Radnorshire, one of the literary clerics in whom we shared an interest. When I was looking into the life of Georg Sauerwein, the Welsh-speaking polyglot who worked for the British and Foreign Bible Society and was a friend of Lady Llanover, it was to her I turned. Our acquaintance was not dented even after 1967 when I, with others, recommended the winding up of *Undeb Cymru Fydd*, the organization to which she and her husband had long been devoted, on the grounds that it had outlived its usefulness – I think she concurred.

Mari Ellis's editorial ability is to be seen at its best in *Y Golau Gwan*, a selection of love-letters written by her father-in-law, T.E. Ellis, to his wife Annie in which the Zeitgeist of Liberal Wales, with its high hopes for an overwhelmingly Nonconformist nation, shines from every page. She was devoted to the memory of T. E. Ellis, who stood for so many of the ideals that she herself embraced, not least the legislative assembly which he postulated in a famous speech at Bala in 1890 when accepting a national testimonial from the people of Wales.

It was a source of great satisfaction to Mari Ellis that her daughter Marged Dafydd (Meg Ellis), while inheriting her grandfather's and father's love of books, also kicked over the family traces and threw herself into the rumbustious but non-violent activities of *Cymdeithas yr Iaith Gymraeg* which from its inception in 1962 challenged the London government and local authorities to provide better provision for Welsh in such sectors as the law, education and broadcasting, its members often breaking the law in order to make their point and then facing the consequences in the form of fines and imprisonment.

One of Marged Dafydd's novels, *I'r Gad* (1975), takes the form of a prison diary and another, *Cyn Daw'r Gaeaf* (1985), is a diary of the women's peace protests at Greenham Common against its use as an American airbase. Mari Ellis, like her daughter, was often to be seen carrying a placard and wrote eloquently in defence of the young people who were dragged before the courts or fell foul of their employers as a consequence of their militancy. She thought it better to light a small candle than to curse the dark.

Mary (Mari) Gwendoline Headley, writer and historian: born Dylife, Montgomeryshire, 21 July 1913; married 1949 Thomas Iorwerth Ellis (died 1970; one son, one daughter); died Aberystwyth, 25 January 2015.

The Independent (15 March 2015)

D. ELLIS EVANS

Acclaimed scholar of Celtic

THE PROFESSOR OF Celtic at Jesus College, Oxford, from 1978 to 1996, D. Ellis Evans took as the field of his research the culture of the early continental Celts, particularly its relationship with that of the classical world, and the history of the insular Celtic languages, especially Welsh and Irish, and their literatures.

He will be remembered mainly on account of his *Gaulish Personal Names: a study of some Continental Celtic Formations*, which appeared in 1967, a magisterial work of immense scholarship that explores the foundations of European civilization and remains the standard book on its subject.

Evans was the fourth occupant of the Chair of Celtic at Oxford, the oldest of its kind in Britain, succeeding Sir Idris Foster, his compatriot, who had been in post for some 30 years, and like him was responsible for supervising the research of postgraduates, work which he undertook with uncommon zeal. Unlike Foster, however, he did not much enjoy the 'high table' pleasures of collegiate life but preferred to pursue his own academic interests. He was the author of numerous scholarly articles in learned periodicals in both Welsh and English, and contributed regularly to such prestigious international journals as *Studia Celtica*, *Études Celtiques* and *Zeitschrift für Celtische Philologie*.

He also edited *Agricola*, a laudatory monograph by Tacitus on the life of his father-in-law, Julius Agricola, written about AD 98. It is of special interest to Celticists because it recounts Agricola's early military service in Britain in the troubled times when Suetonius Paulinus was governor (the days of

Boudicca) and describes the island's tribes and their conquest by the Romans.

David Ellis Evans was born in 1930 at Llanfynydd in Carmarthenshire. His elder brother, Simon, who died in 1998, became Professor of Welsh at University College, Dublin, Head of the Department of Celtic Studies at Liverpool University and was Professor of Welsh at St David's University College, Lampeter, from 1974 to 1988.

Like his brother, Ellis Evans received his secondary education as a boarder at the county school in Llandeilo, where he was unhappy on account of the anglicized atmosphere of both school and town, especially after the outbreak of war when an army camp was opened in the vicinity. After a year at the University College of Wales, Aberystwyth, and following the death of his father, he moved to University College, Swansea, where he graduated with a First in Greek, Latin and Welsh.

As a postgraduate student who went up to Jesus College on a Meyricke Scholarship in 1952, he was among the first to be supervised by Idris Foster. He also threw himself into the activities of the Dafydd ap Gwilym Society, founded in 1886 and still the principal meeting-place for Welsh men and women at Oxford. He returned to Oxford in 1978, after teaching in the Welsh Department at Swansea, where he had been promoted professor in 1974, and remained at Jesus until his retirement in 1996. Among the duties in which he took keenest pleasure was chairing the Dafydd, as it has been affectionately known among generations of its members; with R. Brinley Jones he edited a charming monograph on the Society, *Cofio'r Dafydd* (1987).

He held many offices in the life of the university and beyond its walls. He served as Chairman of the Faculty of Medieval and Modern Languages, curator of the Taylor Institution, secretary of the 7th International Congress of Celtic Studies which took place in Oxford in 1983 and of the North American Celtic Studies Congress held in Ottawa in

1986. He was also a member of the International Committee of Onomastic Sciences, the Irish Texts Society, the Council for Name Studies of Great Britain and Ireland and the UNESCO International Committee for the Study of Celtic Cultures.

In Wales he was Vice-President of the Clwyd Place-Name Council, Chairman of the Welsh Dialect Studies Group, a governor of St David's College, Brecon, and a member of the Welsh Arts Council and the Royal Commission on Ancient and Historical Monuments. He was also editor of the language and literature section of the *Bulletin of the Board of Celtic Studies* from 1973 to 1993. A Festschrift, including a bibliography, was published in his honour under the title *Hispano-Gallo-Britonnica* (ed. R. Geraint Gruffydd et al.) in 1995.

Unlike many other distinguished scholars, including his predecessor, Ellis Evans played no part in the affairs of the National Eisteddfod, although he was elected to the White Robe of the Gorsedd of Bards by virtue of his standing as Jesus Professor of Celtic. Nor did he seek the limelight on Welsh radio and television. Indeed, he was not at all well known in Wales, except among a small circle of scholars and friends from his Swansea days. But there was nothing of the ivory tower about him and, an amiable man, he took great delight in the company of his colleagues and students.

David Ellis Evans, Celtic scholar: born Llanfynydd, Carmarthenshire, 23 September 1930; Lecturer and Professor of Welsh, University College, Swansea 1957–78; Jesus Professor of Celtic, University of Oxford 1978–96 and Emeritus; married 1957 Sheila Jeremy (two daughters); died 26 September 2013.

The Independent (3 November 2013)

MEREDYDD EVANS

Writer and broadcaster who devoted his life
and career to the cultural and linguistic health of Wales

THERE SEEMED TO be more than one Meredydd Evans. So numerous were his talents, and so prodigally did he scatter them, that his name crops up in discussion of almost every sphere of Welsh cultural life from folk-music and philosophy to broadcasting and language politics.

Not for him the narrow specialism of Academe or the dull routine of corporate bureaucracy, though he taught Philosophy at Boston University and, from 1963 to 1973, was Head of Light Entertainment at BBC Wales. Nor was he averse to mixing the highly serious with the genuinely popular: he wrote an acclaimed study of the Scottish philosopher David Hume but also, in a light tenor voice, sang some of the most charming songs ever heard on Welsh radio, earning (much to his chagrin) the accolade 'the Welsh Bing'.

He composed the haunting music for *'Colli Iaith'*, a patriotic poem by Harri Webb which has been sung so many times that it has achieved the status of a traditional air, and also wrote extensively on the *plygain* carols (perhaps from the Latin *pulli cantus*, cock crow), sung in the early hours of Christmas morning since pre-Reformation times, notably in northern Montgomeryshire. The full range of his singing is to be heard on the double CD entitled *Merêd* which was released in 2005, when it became generally known that he was suffering from cancer.

If he did not give his whole mind either to philosophy or to entertainment for long, it was because he saw the need to work on a broad front and was not at all bothered when his friends complained that as a philosopher he was not serious enough and as an entertainer, too much so. Be that as it may, his achievements in both fields were substantial.

It says much for Meredydd Evans's commitment to Welsh, his first language, that he put his career in jeopardy by his support for *Cymdeithas yr Iaith Gymraeg*, which since 1962 has campaigned, often controversially but always by non-violent methods, for greater recognition of Welsh in the public life of Wales, especially in its attempts to persuade representatives of central government to give the language a measure of official status in Wales.

This militancy, and his unflagging support for language campaigners in court and gaol, almost certainly cost him the job of Controller of BBC Wales, for which he was hotly tipped, and made him something of a *bête noire* in Establishment circles.

Undeterred, in 1980, together with two other senior academics, namely Ned Thomas and Pennar Davies, he broke into and switched off a television transmitter at Pencarreg in Carmarthenshire in a symbolic protest against the Conservative government dragging its feet over the establishment of S4C, the fourth television channel.

For his speech from the dock, a classic statement of Welsh nationalism, which in his case was grounded in the language, he won a wide measure of admiration from young activists; his action also prompted Saunders Lewis, the veteran writer and early leader of Plaid Cymru, to write a memorable squib celebrating the occasion.

But during the late 1990s the channel proved a disappointment to Meredydd Evans, as to many others who had expected a wholly Welsh service. He grew ever more critical of it, mainly on account of its readiness to allow a certain amount of English in its Welsh-language programmes, arguing from the fundamental principle that the Welsh-speaker has a moral right to a full service in his or her own language. The Broadcasting Act of 1980, which had paved the way for the creation of S4C, and for which thousands of Welsh-speakers had struggled long and hard, was being observed, he thought, as much in the breach as in the observance.

He remained an unrelenting critic of those at the channel's helm and, as a leading member of *Cylch yr Iaith*, a small but staunchly motivated band of mainly middle-aged people spearheading the campaign against the intrusion of English on Welsh radio and television, also took on BBC Cymru, monitoring its output and challenging its every attempt to justify its policies. He was fined more than once for refusing to pay for a television licence, managing to escape prison only after unidentified supporters paid the fines on his behalf.

His last skirmish, interrupted only by ill health and surgery, was mounted in a forlorn attempt to dissuade the mandarins of Welsh broadcasting from using material by non-Welsh artists, against the trend now firmly established in the Welsh pop industry.

Although he was an effective public speaker, there was nothing of the firebrand about Merêd, as he was generally known in Wales: the gentlest of zealots, and the most amiable of men, he always argued from the highest intellectual ground and in a dignified manner which most broadcasting executives found, if not wholly convincing, quite disconcerting.

Meredydd Evans, a native of Llanegryn in Meirionnydd, was brought up at Tanygrisiau in the slate-quarrying district of Blaenau Ffestiniog. Having been obliged by his father's ill health to leave school at the age of 14, he worked for seven years in the local Co-op, and entered the University College of North Wales, Bangor, in 1940, taking a First in Philosophy. From there he went to Princeton University, where he was awarded his doctorate, and from 1955 to 1960 he taught at Boston, where in 1957 the students voted him Professor of the Year. During his sojourn in the United States he met both Albert Einstein and Marilyn Monroe.

It was in the United States that he met and married Phyllis Kinney, a professional opera-singer from Michigan, who learned Welsh to perfection and shared his keen interest in traditional folk-song. They collaborated in research and the publication of books and records which were as entertaining as they were informative, the songs, both Welsh and American, often illustrated by duets notable for their clarity of diction and an infallible sense of the authentic flavour of the music. The *Folkways* album he brought out in 1954 was selected by *The New York Times* as one of the dozen best folk records released that year.

Meredydd Evans had first made his name as an accomplished vocalist while still an undergraduate at Bangor, where he and two friends formed the close-harmony group known as *Triawd y Coleg*. Whenever they sang in the programme *Noson Lawen*, it was said that the streets of north Wales emptied for half an hour or so. The group gave him his first taste of broadcasting and he became a regular participant in radio programmes, both as singer and presenter. In 1963 he left his post as tutor in the Department of Adult Education at Bangor to become Head of Light Entertainment with BBC Wales in Cardiff.

The ten years he spent with the BBC were fruitful but not without their frustrations. He was responsible for a number of popular programmes featuring the comic genius Ryan Davies, notably *Fo a Fe*, in which a beery, loquacious, lurcher-loving, Marxist collier from south Wales, played by Davies, came into weekly conflict with a sanctimonious, organ-playing, teetotal, Liberal deacon from the north played by Guto Roberts. The series, for all its stereotypes and broad farce, was roughly the equivalent on the laughter-scale to *Steptoe and Son* and is regularly repeated as one of the finest productions from 'the golden age' of Welsh light entertainment. He was also largely responsible for the explosion of Welsh pop music during the 1960s.

But Meredydd Evans was too much of a rebel, or perhaps

not pin-striped enough, to be a Corporation man and, denied the resources he required to make programmes of quality, turned his back on broadcasting in 1973 to take up a post as tutor in the Department of Extra-Mural Studies at University College, Cardiff, where he remained until his retirement in 1985.

He now turned to writing for the Welsh academic press, in particular *Y Traethodydd* and *Efrydiau Athronyddol*, the venerable journal published by the philosophy section of the Guild of Graduates of the University of Wales. In nothing he wrote did he make any concession to the reader looking for simplification of complex matters but in his study of the sceptic Hume, published in 1984, he discussed with great lucidity the nature of knowledge and, *inter alia*, the principle of cause and effect.

His own religious beliefs were Christian but unorthodox. In an interview broadcast by S4C in 1984 and remarkable for its frank references to his own shortcomings, which included a short fuse when dealing with those in authority, he explained how he had thought himself unworthy of the ministry he had at first contemplated, how his reading of Hume had made him ever more questioning, and how he had struggled to regain his faith under the influence of W.T. Stace, one of his professors at Princeton. Even so, he found it hard to accept the Incarnation, preferring to believe in God *through* Jesus Christ rather than *in* Him.

At the heart of his political beliefs was the Welsh language, which he saw as a bastion against the grey uniformity imposed by the authoritarian State. He explored this problem in the conviction that the dissident is a key figure in the contemporary world and, in the Welsh context, that the defence of the national identity against the centralism of the British State is a condition of civilization in its fullest sense. He left the Labour Party and joined Plaid Cymru in 1960.

Among the writers with whose work he engaged in reviews, articles and lectures were William Williams, the hymn-writer known as Pantycelyn who was the harbinger of Romanticism in Welsh poetry, Kate Roberts, generally regarded as the greatest Welsh prose-writer of the twentieth century, the agnostic poet and essayist T.H. Parry-Williams, and the Catholic playwright Saunders Lewis, whom he defended against charges of anti-Semitism. His major lecture on civil disobedience, in which he explored the example of Gandhi and its relevance to Wales, appeared in *Efrydiau Athronyddol* in 1994, and in the same year a selection from his prodigious output of scholarly writings was also published.

His second venture into print journalism was the part he played, in 1973, in launching *Y Dinesydd*, a monthly freebie for the 30,000 Welsh-speakers in Cardiff which still flourishes. Relying for its early success on his enthusiasm and editorial expertise, it was the first of some 50 community newspapers, written entirely in Welsh, which are now published in most parts of Wales.

What drove Meredydd Evans in his tireless campaign against the anglicization of Wales, besides what he saw as the shortcomings of the broadcasting authorities, was the influx of English people into the Welsh-speaking heartlands in the north and west of the country.

He had first-hand experience of this problem after he left Cardiff to live in Cwmystwyth, a village a little to the south of Aberystwyth and in a district fast losing its Welsh under pressure from English incomers. The social fabric of the valley was being adversely affected by the growing number of second homes and retired Midlanders who seemed unaware of the damage their presence and attitudes were doing to the indigenous culture.

In 1987, from the stage of the National Eisteddfod, he spoke out with typical fearlessness against local authorities which allowed this to happen, for which he was accused of being anti-English in some quarters. Many shared his view, but he was the first to express it so forthrightly and his declaration, couched as it was in reasonable and elegant language, stimulated discussion of this vexed question which has still to work itself out in practical terms.

The great affection in which he and his wife were held, together with a full bibliography of his extensive writings, is evident from the essays gathered in the volume *Cynheiliaid y Gân / Bearers of Song* (2007). He was presented with the World Wide Wales Award in 2010.

Like the Wittgensteinian philosopher J.R. Jones, whom he admired, Meredydd Evans saw the Welsh identity as an amalgam of land and language: 'It is said of one experience that it is among the most agonizing of all, namely that of having to leave the soil of one's country for ever, of being torn away by the roots from your homeland. I have not suffered that experience, but I know of another which is just as painful and more irreversible, and that is knowing not that you are leaving your country but that your country is leaving you, is ceasing to exist under your very feet, sucked away from you as if by an insatiable, consuming wind, into the hands and possession of another country, another civilisation.'

Meredydd Evans, broadcaster, teacher and Welsh-language activist: born Llanegryn, Meirionnydd, 9 December 1919; Professor of Philosophy, Boston University, 1955–60; Tutor in the Department of Adult Education, University College of North Wales, Bangor, 1960–63; Head of Light Entertainment, BBC Wales, 1963–73; Tutor in the Department of Extra-Mural Studies, University College, Cardiff, 1973–85; married 1948 Phyllis Kinney (one daughter); died Aberystwyth, Ceredigion, 21 February 2015.

The Independent (19 April 2015)

LLION GRIFFITHS

Editor of *Y Cymro*

LLION GRIFFITHS WAS appointed editor of *Y Cymro* in 1966 and remained in post with the weekly paper for 22 years. The 1960s in Wales, as elsewhere, were a decade of social protest that challenged the bearded orthodoxies as never before, reshaping the Welsh people's understanding of themselves and the wider world. Young Welsh-speakers went in for demonstrations, sit-ins, hunger-strikes, marches, the obliteration of English-only road-signs and a variety of other law-breaking activities which often led to fines and prison sentences.

But the event that caused most controversy and ill feeling was the investiture in July 1969 at Caernarfon castle of the Prince of Wales, a hotly disputed title that offended many Welsh people's sense of history and seemed to represent the English ascendancy in its crassest form.

It was the decision to allow the prince to address the eisteddfod of *Urdd Gobaith Cymru* (the youth movement) that brought matters to a head, as far as Llion Griffiths was concerned. About a hundred people in the front rows, some carrying placards, walked out of the pavilion just as the prince was about to speak. A lame attempt by an *Urdd* official to make light of the incident by pointing out that more people had remained in their seats than had walked out made the editor see red.

He had, up to then, been only mildly critical of the decision to involve the prince and had remained on the fence in the heated controversy that ensued. But now he became strongly averse to such politicians as George Thomas, then Secretary of State for Wales, and many members of the Welsh Establishment who had joined in the ceremonies.

What's more, he began criticising the investiture in *Y Cymro*, seeing it as a celebration of England's conquest of Wales. In his first editorial after the walkout, he reminded readers that the protest had been non-violent, silent and altogether dignified. A man of great principle, he could not bring himself to condemn the principled stand consistently taken by the dissenters.

But in the week of the investiture itself, the lead story in *Y Cymro* was the gaoling of several members of the Free Wales Army, their trial having been arranged to coincide with the ceremony at Caernarfon.

This was a hazardous line for the editor to take. The newspaper was owned at the time by Woodalls, a company with offices over the border in Oswestry and its directors' appreciation of Welsh-language militancy and the paper's role in the culture of Wales was not to the fore. But whatever blandishments they may have made, it did not deter the editor from supporting the Welsh Language Society (founded in 1962) in all its subsequent campaigns over the next 20 years.

Llion Griffiths had but little formal training as a journalist. Born in the hamlet of Glanyrafon, near Bala in Meirionnydd, he studied at the Theological College in Aberystwyth with a view to joining the ministry but, once qualified, changed his mind and took a job with the Farmers' Union of Wales.

He undertook his editorial duties with flair and panache, strengthening the news-gathering methods of a newspaper which had begun to see its role challenged by television and its production costs soaring. He gave pages to pop culture, sport and motoring, and found room for lots more photos and cartoons, so that *Y Cymro*, founded in 1932, widened its appeal as a family newspaper while still holding up a mirror to the social and political life of Wales, and its weekly circulation rose. He was greatly respected by younger journos, many of whom were taken under his wing.

Having relinquished the editorial chair in 1988, Griffiths stayed on as business manager for another seven years, using his many contacts in all parts of Wales to garner much-needed revenue in the form of advertisements from public bodies. Although he had successfully negotiated an offer of subsidy from the Welsh Arts Council, it was blocked by the proprietors who thought it inappropriate that a newspaper should take grant-aid from a public body; the paper later received a grant from the Welsh Books Council for its book pages, but was wound up in 2018.

A mild-mannered and genial man, Griffiths was known to have strong convictions, both political and religious, and he was willing to put them into practice. He also had a personal interest in Welsh poetry and, unusually for a journalist, wrote several well-known hymns.

Dewi Llion Griffiths, editor of Y Cymro, *1966–88, and advertisements manager, 1988–95: born Glanyrafon, Meirionnydd, 26 March 1930; married 1956 Mary Price (deceased; one son, one daughter); died Bala, Gwynedd, 2 October 2013.*

R. GERAINT GRUFFYDD

Foremost scholar of the Reformation in Wales

GERAINT GRUFFYDD HELD some of the most prestigious posts in Welsh academic and cultural life, not least the Chair of Welsh at Aberystwyth and that of National Librarian. In 1985 he was appointed director of the University of Wales Centre for Advanced Welsh and Celtic Studies, a post from which he retired in 1993. His most important contribution to Welsh scholarship was his work on the prose written during the Protestant Reformation and on the early Puritans.

Born in 1928 at Tal-y-bont in Meirionnydd, the son of a well-to-do farmer, Moses Griffith, who was the first treasurer of Plaid Cymru and friend of the party's founder Saunders Lewis, Geraint was educated at village schools and then went up to the University College of North Wales, Bangor, and in 1948 on to Jesus College, Oxford, of which he became an Honorary Fellow in 1992. While at Oxford, he became acquainted with Sheldon Vanauken, the American author, a friend of C.S. Lewis, who mentioned him in his book *A Severe Mercy* (1977).

His first job was that of assistant editor with *Geiriadur Prifysgol Cymru / A Dictionary of the Welsh Language*, organised on historical principles like the *OED* but also serving as a monolingual Welsh as well as a bilingual Welsh-English dictionary, a huge project launched in 1921 and still ongoing under the auspices of the University of Wales. But he stayed for only two years before his appointment to a lectureship in Welsh at Bangor in 1955, a promotion which was to set the course of his subsequent career. He moved to Aberystwyth in 1970 as Professor of Welsh language and literature, soon establishing himself as a scholar and critic in his chosen field. Ten years later he became librarian at the National Library of Wales, his genial personality and high standards winning him the respect of his staff and all who used that centre of learning.

Besides a plethora of articles on the major figures of the late Renaissance and Reformation in Wales, in particular the early humanists who placed an emphasis on God's sovereign grace, justification by faith alone, the priesthood of all believers and the authority of God's Word, Geraint also wrote about Dafydd ap Gwilym, generally regarded as the greatest Welsh poet of the medieval period, and on Aneirin, one of the poets who flourished in 'the Old North' (what are today parts of northern England and southern Scotland) in the sixth century. He was general editor of the series *Beirdd y Tywysogion* (7 vols., 1991–96), a field in which he was renowned for his encyclopaedic knowledge and meticulous scholarship, and contributed to *Beirdd yr Uchelwyr* on the poets Meilyr Brydydd, Llywelyn Fardd, Dafydd Benfras and Bleddyn Fardd.

His interests extended to early Welsh printers, the subject of his inaugural lecture at Aberystwyth, subsequently published as *Argraffwyr Cyntaf Cymru* (1972) and to the prose writings of his father's old friend, Saunders Lewis, whose literary essays he edited under the title *Meistri'r Canrifoedd* (1973). Despite his critical approach to the Roman Catholicism of Saunders Lewis, he was one of the trustees of the memorial fund established in the writer's name. He also edited a Festschrift for J.E. Caerwyn Williams, his predecessor at the Centre for Advanced Welsh and Celtic Studies, and was for many years an associate editor of the *Oxford Dictionary of National Biography*.

To the compendium *A Guide to Welsh Literature c.1530–1700* (1997), which he edited, he contributed an exemplary chapter on Anglican prose of the period. Among his lesser works were a study of Daniel Owen, the first great Welsh novelist, and a discussion of Gruffudd ab yr Ynad Coch's powerful elegy for Llywelyn II, the last prince of independent Wales, killed by Anglo-Norman forces at Cilmeri in 1282. He also wrote lucidly on William Morgan, translator of the Bible into Welsh (The Henry Lewis Memorial Lecture, 1989) and in the same year put together an attractively illustrated account of Welsh literature.

The range and quality of Geraint's writing were reflected in the volume *Beirdd a Thywysogion* (ed. Morfydd E. Owen and Brynley F. Roberts), a collection of essays presented to him in 1996. His own essays on literary and religious subjects, many of which first appeared in *Y Cylchgrawn Efengylaidd*, were collected in *Y Ffordd Gadarn* (2008). He was a staunch Calvinist and a leading light in the Evangelical wing of that Connexion, bringing to his fundamentalist faith a keen intelligence that he allowed to play over a wide field of disciplines. With the late R. Tudur Jones, he was the foremost scholar of the Reformation in Wales and a literary critic of rare distinction.

It was inevitable that such a well-equipped scholar should be asked to serve on the myriad committees by which the cultural life of Wales is run. These included the Welsh Academy, the Welsh Books Council, the University of Wales Press Board, the Board of Celtic Studies, the Court of the University College of Wales, Aberystwyth, of which he was Vice-President, the Honourable Society of Cymmrodorion, and the International Congress of Celtic Studies, which he served as President. He was elected Fellow of the British Academy in 1991.

Robert Geraint Gruffydd, scholar and literary critic: born Tal-y-bont, Meirionnydd, 9 June 1928; Lecturer in Welsh, University College of North Wales, Bangor, 1955–70; Professor of Welsh, University College of Wales, Aberystwyth, and Emeritus, 1970–80; Librarian, National Library of Wales, 1980–85; Director, University of Wales Centre for Advanced Welsh and Celtic

Studies, 1985–93; Fellow of the British Academy, 1991; married 1953 Eluned Roberts (two sons, one daughter); died Aberystwyth, 24 March 2015.

The Independent (22 June 2015)

JOHN HEFIN

Film-maker whose work celebrated Wales and its people

FOR AS LONG as rugby is the Welsh national game the film that celebrates it most memorably will be *Grand Slam*, made for BBC Wales in 1978 by the distinguished director John Hefin.

It stars the Oscar-winning Hugh Griffith as Caradog Lloyd-Evans, a lugubrious, lecherous undertaker leading a group of innocents on a trip to Paris, ostensibly to see an international between Wales and France but actually to rekindle the ardour of former days in the arms of the woman with whom he had a fling during the last months of the war. His priapic son Glyn is played by the comic genius Dewi Morris, the camp boutique-owner Maldwyn Novello-Pugh by Siôn Probert, the gorgeous Odette, daughter of Caradog's 'little butterfly', by Sharon Morgan, and the hapless Mog Jones by Windsor Davies. John Hefin encouraged them all to ad-lib, often with hilarious consequences.

Mog's cry of 'Wa-ales! Wa-ales!' through the bars of his cell where he has been locked up by gendarmes for causing an affray, thus missing the game, is enough to bring tears to the eyes. Eventually released by his mystified gaolers, he staggers through the crowded Paris streets in his red vest and boxer shorts and into an empty Parc des Princes echoing with the roar of the long-departed crowd.

Although John Hefin was always a self-effacing man, he could not resist the temptation of emulating his hero Alfred Hitchcock by appearing very briefly in his own film: the attentive viewer will see him emerging from a pissoir and shaking his leg as he leaves. It is one of the many delicious details that give the film its evergreen appeal.

John, who wrote the script of *Grand Slam* with Gwenlyn Parry, first in Welsh and then in English, made the film into one of the iconic images of Welsh life by training a knowing but affectionate eye on the feverish sensibilities of his countrymen whenever the national side is called upon to defend the honour of Wales.

His name will be forever linked with the laughter and pathos of the event, especially after Wales lose the match and the crestfallen fans make their way home. He made defeat seem sweet to a people who have learned, over the centuries, to make the most of it, and the film was taken to his compatriots' hearts as the funniest film ever made about rugby.

It was said that wives wouldn't let their husbands go on trips to Paris after *Grand Slam*. The mother of Dewi Morris would not go to chapel in Treboeth after seeing him cavorting with a naked Odette (albeit with one eye on the match on a television set in her bedroom) until the minister informed her it was one of the funniest things he'd seen on television in years, after which she basked in his overnight fame.

The film was not John Hefin's only achievement. In September 1974, he devised a soap opera for the BBC, *Pobol y Cwm*. It was originally intended to run for only ten episodes but it was an immediate hit, and remains a firm favourite, with Welsh audiences.

Set in the village of Cwmderi, somewhere between Carmarthen and Llanelli – although now filmed in purpose-built studios in Cardiff Bay – the series, which is to be seen nightly on S4C, has had a huge effect on television ratings in Wales, as most successful soaps do, and is now a cornerstone of the service. The use of subtitles attracts many English-speaking viewers who are among the show's most enthusiastic fans.

It has also played an important role in providing actors, writers and camera crews with opportunities for earning a living through the medium of the Welsh language, which has proved flexible and capacious enough to accommodate the new technology.

John Hefin made a deliberate attempt from the outset to appeal to the whole of Wales by creating characters from all parts of the country so that the main regional accents are to be heard in the dialogue. His vision and determination to lay the foundations of popular broadcasting in Welsh, his first language to which he was zealously committed, cannot be over-emphasized.

During his time as Head of Drama at the BBC, a role in which he preferred original plays to adaptations, he produced and directed some of the finest home-grown programmes ever seen in Wales. They include *Bus to Bosworth*, in which the quirky Kenneth Griffith takes a busload of schoolchildren to visit the scene of Henry Tudor's victory over Richard III in 1485, *Tough Trade*, starring Anthony Hopkins, *O.M.*, about the great patriot O.M. Edwards, and *Mr Lollipop M.A.* in which Flora Robson had a part. He once told me the Bosworth film, which he scripted, was meant to be a tribute to his father who, as headmaster at the village school in Tre Taliesin, used to organize bus-trips for his pupils to places of historical interest.

His most controversial production was *The Mimosa Boys* (1985), which challenged the official version of the bombing of the *Sir Galahad* and the loss of Welsh soldiers in the Falklands campaign. Based largely on interviews with survivors, the script by Ewart Alexander focused on the lives of four young men immediately before embarkation and was a creditable attempt to provide an unblinkered account of the tragedy. But opinion was divided: was the film a radical critique of military tactics that left men unprotected or a homage to their courage under fire?

His other major achievement was undoubtedly *The Life and Times of David Lloyd George*, in which the statesman was played by Philip Madoc. The biopic's script was by Elaine Morgan and the series had haunting theme-music by Ennio

Morricone, whose 'Chi Mai' sequence became a surprise hit in the UK charts.

John Hefin went into semi-retirement in the 1990s but joined the staff of the University College of Wales in his home town to create a course in film and television studies, where he proved to be an inspirational Teaching Fellow. He was also a Fellow of the Welsh College of Music and Drama in Cardiff.

A man of great charm and broad culture, he was prepared to roll up his sleeves and work hard in the interests of broadcasting in Wales. He played a leading role in setting up the South Wales Film Commission and was Chairman of *Cyfrwng*, the body that promotes inter-disciplinary debate about the media in Wales. In recognition of his services to the industry, he received a major prize from *Cyfrwng* in July 2012. He was also awarded an MBE and admitted to the prestigious Gorsedd of Bards.

Although never politically active, it was he, with his lifelong friend David Meredith, later Head of Press and Public Relations with HTV and S4C, who in 1962 painted the word 'Elis' on a large boulder near the Pumlumon road that leads down to Aberystwyth, as publicity for Islwyn Ffowc Elis, the Plaid Cymru candidate at a forthcoming by-election in Montgomeryshire. Days later it was changed by an unknown hand to 'Elvis' and 'the Elvis Rock' became a landmark that went on amusing motorists for years thereafter. John savoured the joke as much as anyone.

John Hefin Evans, film-maker: born Aberystwyth, Cardiganshire, 14 August 1941; married first Non Watkin Jones (marriage dissolved, one son, one daughter); secondly Elin Williams (one daughter); died Borth, Ceredigion, 19 November 2012.

The Independent (5 December 2012)

GLYN TEGAI HUGHES

Esteemed literary critic and first warden of Gregynog Hall

GLYN TEGAI HUGHES combined a profound knowledge of writing in the Welsh language with a keen interest in the literature of Germany and Switzerland, especially from the Romantic period, and was able to make comparative judgements which cast light on both.

He was also a bibliophile and collector of fine editions, an interest which he was able to pursue as warden of Gregynog Hall, the University of Wales residential centre near Newtown in the old county of Montgomeryshire, now part of Powys, where he was instrumental in reviving the celebrated Gregynog Press.

Glyn Tegai, as he was known in Wales, was perhaps the most cerebral of critics and the most ascetic of book-men, but it did not prevent him from playing a part in the public affairs of Wales, notably as National Governor and Chairman of the Broadcasting Council for Wales from 1971 to 1979.

He was born in Chester in 1923, the son of the Reverend John Hughes, a Wesleyan minister, whose peripatetic mission ensured that the family did not stay long in any one place but moved from chapel to chapel throughout the length and breadth of Wales. The question 'Where do you come from?', often asked in Wales, bothered Glyn Tegai, for he was at a loss to say where his roots lay.

After receiving his secondary education at county schools in Newtown, Towyn and Brynmawr, at the Liverpool Institute and Manchester Grammar School, he went up to Corpus Christi, Cambridge, where he was the Donaldson Scholar, took first-class honours in Modern Languages Tripos, and was then awarded his doctorate.

From 1942 to 1946 he served as captain and then temporary major with the Royal Welch Fusiliers and was the deputy assistant adjutant general in the South-East Asia Command. One of Mountbatten's 'bright boys', he retained a great affection for Malaysia, Singapore and Sri Lanka for the rest of his life.

The direction of his academic career was set when he was appointed Lektor in English literature at the University of Basel in 1952. It was there he discovered an interest in the work of the Swiss Protestant pastor Jeremias Gotthelf (1797–1854), whose novels of Emmental life held great appeal for him.

He wrote two books on German literature: *Eichendorff's Taugenichts* (1961), a study of the short novel *Aus dem Leben eines Taugenichts* (1826) by J.F. von Eichendorff (1788–1857), and *Romantic German Literature* (1979), a useful short guide to its subject.

Before returning to Wales as the first warden of Gregynog in 1964, Glyn Tegai Hughes spent 11 years at the University of Manchester, first as lecturer in comparative literary studies and then as tutor in the faculty of arts.

At Gregynog he immersed himself in the history of the old house and its former owners, the spinster sisters Margaret and Gwendoline Davies, whose generous bequest to the University of Wales it had been, and set about re-organizing its library and re-planning its 750 acres. It was he who set the tone of the country-house ambience which so many visitors to Gregynog, however briefly, have subsequently enjoyed.

Those attending courses at the hall were always entertained by the warden, at dinner on the first evening, who would give a witty and sometimes sardonic account of the place in the sisters' day, with cameo sketches of such people as Thomas Jones (1870–1955), the Machiavellian civil servant whose judgement in the appointment of staff and the purchase of paintings, including some important Impressionist works, was the only one they trusted. One of Glyn's favourite anecdotes was that, in the days when Gregynog had its own choir, the sisters, at Jones's bidding, used to advertise for gardeners with the words 'Tenors preferred'.

Even so, it was to be several years before the abstemious warden, a zealous Wesleyan lay-preacher, would apply for a licence to open a bar at Gregynog, thus obliging some of the more bibulous house-guests to go to ingenious lengths when smuggling in their own bottles. In the early days of his wardenship, the peaty water served at table from a private reservoir behind the house was jocularly known as Château Tegai.

The aspect of his job into which Glyn Tegai threw himself with the greatest gusto was the revival of the Gregynog Press, which had been founded with the millionaire Davies sisters' money in 1923 and was one of the great private presses of the inter-war years. Famous for their bindings, Gregynog books now fetch high prices among dealers and collectors.

At the time, he was Chairman of the Welsh Arts Council's Literature Committee and, as Literature Director, I was an ally in this enterprise. With the council's financial aid, the Press, given the Welsh form of its name, Gwasg Gregynog, took on a new lease of life in 1974 under its Controller Eric Gee and its Chairman, Lord Kenyon.

Glyn Tegai steered the work of the advisory board with a firm but sympathetic hand. Among the first books to be produced was his life of Thomas Olivers (1725–99), the Methodist exhorter born in the nearby village of Tregynon whose hymns 'Come, Immortal King of Glory' and 'The God of Abram praise' are still sung by Wesleyan congregations.

With David Esslement, the second controller under the new dispensation, the warden also wrote a descriptive catalogue of the Press (1990) in which his pleasure in typography, fine printing, binding and illustration was given full rein.

By the time he retired in 1989 the Press had published, besides many smaller productions, a number of large-scale books which compared well with those made at Gregynog in its heyday. They included works by R.S. Thomas, Francis Kilvert, Kate Roberts, Robert Williams Parry, Saunders Lewis, Giraldus Cambrensis, Stephen Crane and Dylan Thomas, all of which are now out of print.

On the occasion of his retirement the Board presented Glyn Tegai with a copy, in quarter-leather, of *Hugo Wolf Lieder after poems by Eduard Mörike*, printed on Japanese Gampi vellum in Trump Mediaeval, his favourite typeface, of which only 30 copies were made. The distinguished printers Brooke Crutchley and Vivian Ridler were among the 14 subscribers to what must be the rarest piece of ephemera ever produced at Gregynog.

As a literary critic, Glyn Tegai wrote perceptively about Welsh writing in English, notably the novels set in the industrial valleys of south Wales, but his *magnum opus* is the essay he contributed to the *Writers of Wales* series on the great hymn-writer William Williams (1717–91) of Pantycelyn, the man who composed the original Welsh words of the powerful hymn usually sung at rugby-matches as 'Bread of Heaven'.

With Saunders Lewis, he saw Pantycelyn as one of the earliest exponents of Romanticism in European literature, and brought to his reading of the hymns and prose-works several theological insights and a sensitive understanding of the historical and literary background which make this monograph a major contribution to our understanding of the literature of the period.

Politically, Glyn Tegai was a Liberal. He stood as the party's candidate in the West Denbigh division three times between 1950 and 1959, coming a close second to the sitting National Liberal and Conservative members, and was the party's Vice-President for a term.

A close friend of Emlyn Hooson, the Liberal MP for Montgomeryshire from 1962 to 1979, he never wavered in his allegiance to the Liberal cause and spoke from many platforms, as he once told me, 'just to show whose side I am on'. He was a most eloquent speaker, one of the best the Liberal Party has ever had, in the judgement of Lord Hooson when presenting him for an honorary fellowship at the University of Wales, Aberystwyth, in 2000.

He also sat on many committees. As well as serving the BBC as National Governor and Chairman of the Broadcasting Council for Wales, he was Chairman of *Undeb Cymru Fydd* (1968–70), a somewhat forlorn rump of the movement which, in Lloyd George's day, had nearly brought Home Rule to Wales.

He was Vice-President of the North Wales Arts Association (1977–94), President of the Private Libraries Association (1980–82), Chairman of the Welsh Broadcasting Trust (1988–96), and a member of S4C, the fourth television channel in Wales.

To all these posts he brought practical expertise, unusual in one for whom the things of the mind took precedence over mere financial or administrative niceties. Some found him aloof, an impression strengthened by his spare frame and analytical manner, but there was a warmer, more generous side to his character of which he sometimes allowed a glimpse.

On retirement, he went to live at Rhyd-y-gro, a house on the Gregynog estate. But after the death in 1996 of his wife Margaret, an Australian, whom he had met at the World Methodist Conference in the United States in 1956, and with whom he set up the marriage counselling organization Relate in mid Wales, he was seen less frequently around the grounds. He took no further part in public life, content to augment and catalogue his vast personal library and tend the garden shrubs which were one of his few hobbies.

Glyn Tegai Hughes, bibliophile, literary critic and Warden of Gregynog Hall, 1964–89: born Chester, 18 January 1923; married 1957 Margaret Vera Herbert (died 1996; one son and one son deceased); died Tregynon, 10 March 2017.

The Independent (22 May 2017)

NIGEL JENKINS

Politically engaged and outspoken poet

OF ALL WELSH poets writing in English, Nigel Jenkins was one of the most politically engaged and outspoken. His views and actions often got him into hot water. In 1988 he was jailed for seven days for refusing to pay a £40 fine imposed after a protest outside the American airbase at Brawdy, in Pembrokeshire. He had cut the perimeter fence as part of CND's Operation Snowball, a campaign aimed at persuading the government to vote in favour of multilateral disarmament. 'I consider it my duty as a Welshman and an internationalist,' he told reporters, 'to do all in my power to end the continuing presence on Welsh soil of American and British nuclear bases.' In 1987 he co-edited the anthology *Glas-Nos* for CND Cymru.

Nigel believed, unlike Auden, that poetry could make things happen, especially in Wales where poets are often called upon to write verse that inspires the community to take action against overweening officialdom. His poems were meant to offend, and offend they often did. When his 'Execrably Tasteless Farewell to Viscount No' appeared in *The Guardian* in 1997, he was pilloried in all the predictable quarters for satirising George Thomas, the recently deceased Speaker of the House of Commons who had been prominent in the No camp during the Devolution campaign that led to the creation of the Welsh Assembly. It was the vitriolic language that raised most hackles: 'white man's Taff... may his garters garrotte him... the Lord of Lickspit, the grovelsome brown-snout and smiley shyster whose quisling wiles were the shame of Wales...'

Nigel courted controversy as often as possible.

Commissioned (with Menna Elfyn and David Hughes) in 1993 to write site-specific poems for the refurbished city centre in Swansea, his native place, he jumped at the opportunity to give poetry the public profile he believed it should have in the lives of the people. 'It is my fortune,' he wrote, 'to work in a country which, unlike its neighbour to the east, has an unbroken tradition of poetry as a social art.'

But he spoke too soon: most of the one-liners such as 'Remember tomorrow' which were inscribed on benches, flagstones, walls, bollards, signposts and the like, were quickly obliterated or removed – not by vandals or hostile citizens but by employees of the council. When confronted by the irate poet, an official was quoted in *The Independent* as saying, 'People find poetry irrational and strange. They don't understand it. They're frightened by it.'

The irony was that Swansea was to be a City of Literature in 1995. Jenkins had expressed disquiet about the concept long before the spat over the lapidary inscriptions. Unhappy at the exclusion of local writers, he had set up the Swansea Writers and Artists Group (SWAG) to remind the organisers of their existence. In the event, the Year of Literature proved something of a damp squib, little more than an exercise in civic philistinism and internecine strife among the literati. He also served as the first secretary of the Welsh Union of Writers, another campaigning group, but it had little clout with funding bodies.

A man of the Left, his political views found expression in the ranks of Plaid Cymru, and he served on the editorial board of *Radical Wales*, though as a Welsh Republican he sometimes groaned at the party's shortcomings. 'It is difficult to write effective political poetry,' he once told an interviewer, 'in the same way that it must be difficult to write religious poetry, without banging the drum and thumping the tub. I have fallen into such error all too readily. On the other hand, there is scope for the political poem which may not have much of a shelf-life but which has a job to do, gets in there, blazes away and gets out again.'

Nigel Jenkins was born in Gorseinon, Swansea, in 1949 and raised on his parents' farm on the Kilvrough estate in Gower. On leaving school he worked for four years as a newspaper reporter in the English Midlands and then, after wandering in Europe and North Africa, and working as a circus-hand in America, went to study comparative literature and film at the University of Essex. He returned to Wales in 1976, settling in Mumbles on Swansea Bay and earning a living as a freelance writer. With his sonorous voice, the blackest of beards and rugged good looks, he was a popular participant in poetry readings and conferences. A kind, eirenic and selfless man, he was invariably generous in his dealings with other people and especially so with younger writers whom he encouraged and whose work he promoted, so that he was universally liked and admired.

He first came to prominence as one of three young poets named by the Welsh Arts Council in 1974. From the start his concern was with Wales and its place in the world. His poems are in turn local, cosmological, satirical, playful, bitter, comic, ribald, and dismissive. They are to be found for the most part in *Song and Dance* (1981), *Practical Dreams* (1983), *Acts of Union* (1990), *Ambush* (1998), and *Hotel Gwales* (2006). He also published two collections of *haiku*, *senryū* and *tanka*, namely *Blue* (2002) and *O for a gun* (2007), traditional Japanese forms that lend themselves to the concise wit and withering satire of which he was a master.

Two books of prose added cubits to Nigel's literary reputation: *Gwalia in Khasia* (1995) is about Welsh missionaries in the Khasi Hills of north-east India and *Footsore on the Frontier* (2001) brings together a selection of his miscellaneous essays. The first of these, selected as the Wales Book of the Year in 1996, was compared by competent critics to the work of such travel-writers as Jan Morris and Paul Theroux. He also wrote a warmly appreciative monograph on John Tripp, a fellow-poet whose search for any sign of benevolent grace struck a chord with him.

Nigel's work for the theatre included *Waldo's Witness* (Coracle, 1986), about the great pacifist poet Waldo Williams, and *Strike a Light!* (Made in Wales, 1989), about the Chartist and pioneer of cremation, Dr William Price. Two coffee-table books followed: *The Lie of the Land* (with photographer Jeremy Moore, 1996) and *Gower* (with David Pearl, 2009). He also edited the symposium *Thirteen Ways of Looking at Tony Conran* (1995), in homage to a poet he greatly admired, and served as one of the co-editors of *The Encyclopaedia of Wales* (2008). His two books *Real Swansea* (2008, 2009) are a psycho-geography of the 'ugly, lovely' city which he knew in intimate detail. His final book was *Real Gower* (2013), a psycho-geography of his native place.

Nigel Leighton Rowland Jenkins, poet and political activist: born Gorseinon, Swansea, 20 July 1949; married Delyth Evans (marriage dissolved, two daughters); Co-director of the Creative Writing programme, Swansea University; died Swansea, 28 January 2014.

The Independent (12 February 2014)

ANEURIN JONES

Painter who found inspiration in the people of upland mid Wales

IF KYFFIN WILLIAMS was the painter par excellence of the mountains of north Wales, Aneurin Jones, who has died aged 87, took as his subject-matter the people of mid Wales, a landscape less spectacular but no less rugged and, in some respects, just as harsh. He painted the farmers of upland Powys, their hardy womenfolk, their livestock and, in particular, their horses for which he had a special affection. In so doing he recorded a rural society that depended on the small family farm, and felt himself to be the chronicler of a way of life that was fast disappearing.

There is a timelessness about his studies of the mart, the chapel, the sheep-dog trial, the ploughing match, the byre, sheep shearing, the tug o'war, washing day, baking, the harvest supper, the game of draughts, the choir, the public house – all the multifarious activities of a largely self-sufficient community that had remained more or less unchanged for hundreds of years. Although located in the back-country of Breconshire, Carmarthenshire and Cardiganshire, there is too a sense of universality about his work, as if he were painting country folk anywhere in western Europe, a people bent to their daily labours or enjoying rare pleasures, but always yoked to the soil, growing almost organically from the fields and hills that gave them sustenance.

The enormous appeal of his pictures, and his canny policy of keeping his prices within reach of those who do not usually buy contemporary art, made his work extremely popular, especially as he was the product of the Welsh-speaking society he depicted. His strength lay in the fact that he painted people who, despite their universality, were clearly drawn from life, so he could put names to many who sat for him, and sometimes to their dogs and horses too.

Aneurin Jones knew his subject-matter through and through, never tiring of walking the lanes and bridle paths that took him to some of the most remote places in southern Britain, a tract of land which, despite depopulation, retained for him a magical quality. He was never happier than when drawing a man with a scythe cutting grass on a steep slope or a shepherd handling his border collie, observed so vividly that it is almost possible to hear the dog panting and smell the breath from its muzzle.

He was a countryman by birth and upbringing. Born at Pwll Isaf, a small homestead in Cwm Wysg, near Trecastle, on the border of Breconshire and Carmarthenshire, he was familiar not only with the topography of his native patch but also with its history. Not far from his home lay Llyn-y-fan Fach, a lake near Llanddeusant high in the Black Mountains, with its legend of faery cattle thought to have its origin in folk memory dating from the Iron Age.

From the more recent past there were stories of ghostly riders on white horses, chapel preachers, ruined farms, fairs, agricultural shows, ploughing matches, village characters, and Twm Shon Catti, the Welsh Robin Hood, all of which found a place in his paintings, giving them a texture and depth that added to their appeal. Some of his paintings, especially of the trotting Welsh cob and the magnificent shire horse, prompted poets to write verse about them which appeared in his book, *Aneurin* (2000).

There was, too, the memory of the War Office's commandeering of the Epynt to make a firing range, its people having been compulsorily uprooted and their homes destroyed. The ghosts of that unhappy episode from the Second World War still trouble the hills of northern Breconshire: his group of Epynt farmers (1978), in their caps and rough coats, stand idly and awkwardly, as if at a graveside, and in the background is the bare landscape from which they have been evicted.

It was the people, *his* people, that Jones never tired of celebrating. The men and women who appear in his paintings are heroic figures, gnarled by the elements, surviving because of their innate tenacity. There is a titanic quality to many of his labourers, who are caught up in a struggle with a grudging soil and the wind and rain which threaten to strip them of their humanity.

On the other hand, in his domestic scenes there is a gentler touch, as in the pictures of a farm wife feeding her chickens or brushing the floor of her kitchen or hanging out the washing in the yard, all painted about 1983. There is a sincerity and lack of pretension in these lyrical studies which some prefer to the more muscular, heavy-booted men whose large hands grasp their sticks and spades with primeval strength and to whom he returned again and again.

If there is something absent in Jones's canvases it is an awareness of time passing, of changes in country life, of the old order passing and giving place to the new. There are no tractors, combine harvesters, television aerials or motor cars in his pictures and the people are dressed in the earth-coloured clothes of pre-war days. Towards the end of his career the boldly painted figures gave way to a mistier depiction of middle-aged people in passive poses, which suggested that they were waiting for the inevitable end of their way of life. It is as if time, for him, had stopped in the 1950s, when he left home for art college in Swansea. This was a break with his native place from which he never fully recovered and it is possible to see his work as nostalgia, an elegiac lament for what was lost when he left Cwm Wysg.

In Swansea he found he had a special affinity with stained glass and, designing church windows at the Celtic Studios for two years, learned the elements of draughtsmanship which make his pictures so technically pleasing. Although from 1958 to 1986 he earned a living as an art teacher at

Ysgol y Preseli, the comprehensive school in Crymych, Pembrokeshire, where he had the support of an artistically minded headmaster in the person of James Nicholas, he was not a weekend painter and there is nothing amateur about his work. In the Preseli hill-country, land of the Mabinogion tales, he found something of the magic he had once known in Cwm Wysg.

He was not averse to making overtly political statements. One of his most celebrated canvases is the one showing the slogan *'Cofiwch Dryweryn'* (1982) painted on a crumbling barn wall a few miles south of Aberystwyth, a reference to the drowning of the Tryweryn valley to make a reservoir for Liverpool Corporation. In 1994, he painted a large mural for the church at Pennal near Machynlleth which showed Owain Glyndŵr raising the standard of rebellion against the English king. He believed, as a people's remembrancer, that he had a duty to encourage his compatriots to resist the erosion of the Welsh-speaking districts of west and north Wales in the face of English in-migration.

Aneurin – he was known throughout Wales by his first name only – was a small, wiry man, as tough as the hill stock from which he had sprung, with a low chuckle and sparkling eyes, and he enjoyed nothing better than a session of storytelling or a pint in congenial company. He was a regular visitor to the National Eisteddfod and could often be found in the arts and crafts pavilion where he enjoyed the regard of his many admirers. He is survived by his wife Julie, daughter and son Meirion who is also a painter.

Aneurin Morgan Jones, teacher and painter: born Cwm Wysg, Trecastle, Breconshire, 1930; married Julie (one son, one daughter); Head of the Art Department, Ysgol y Preseli, Crymych, Pembrokeshire, 1958–86; died 25 September 2017.

The Independent (1 October 2017)

BOBI (ROBERT MAYNARD) JONES

Scholar of Welsh whose native English became a foreign language

BY FAR THE most prolific Welsh creative writer of the twentieth century, perhaps of all time, Bobi Jones was a man of prodigious energy, immense erudition, fervent religious belief, and passionate commitment to the language, his second language, in which he chose to write more than 60 books – verse, short stories, novels, autobiography, literary criticism and theory, a history of Welsh literature, scholarly editions, linguistic studies, polemical essays, translations, textbooks, and books for teachers and children. This protean output, seen by some as hyperactivity but by the writer as 'the least I could do in the circumstances', intended to be a challenge to those who feared the demise of the Welsh language, a demonstration that it was capable of expressing the complexity of the modern world and the thinking person's place in it. In one of his earliest poems he wrote '*Angau, rwyt ti'n fy ofni i / Am fy mod yn ifanc*' ('Death, you're afraid of me / Because I'm young'), proceeding to flaunt the fecundity of his imagination as proof that the language was alive and kicking; the same defiance and bravado were found in *Rhwng Taf a Thaf* (1960) and *Tyred Allan* (1965). His later poems appear in *Ôl Traed* (2003) and *Yr Amhortreadwy a Phortreadau Eraill* (2009).

Almost as if one name were not sufficient to contain the multiplicity of his talents, he also wrote as R.M. Jones, mainly for the purposes of his scholarly work, which included a primer of critical theory, a study of phonology, morphology and semantics, and four histories of Welsh literature. His book *Cyfriniaeth Gymraeg* (1994) is a study of the connections between religion and Welsh literature, with special reference to the mystical elements in such writers as Morgan Llwyd, William Williams (Pantycelyn), Ann Griffiths, and Waldo Williams, while *Ysbryd y Cwlwm* (1998) examines how Welsh writers have responded to the nationhood of Wales over the centuries. Among other important books, *Mawl a'i Gyfeillion* (2000) is a stimulating study of the bardic tradition, as is its companion volume, *Mawl a Gelynion ei Elynion* (2002). His early writings about critical theory were collected in the volume *Tafod y Llenor* (1974) and under the title *Beirniadaeth Gyfansawdd* (2003). His original thinking about the technicalities of traditional prosody is to be found in *Meddwl y Cynghanedd* (2005).

Robert Maynard Jones was born into an English-speaking home in Cardiff. His family claimed descent from Oliver Cromwell and his grandfather, a Marxist, instilled in him an egalitarian spirit which coloured his early work. At school he learned Welsh and quickly became proficient in it before going on to take a degree in Welsh at the university college in the city. After teaching at schools in Montgomeryshire and Anglesey, and lecturing at Trinity College, Carmarthen, he joined the staff of the Welsh Department in Aberystwyth in 1966; he was appointed Professor of Welsh Language and Literature in 1980 and remained in that post until his retirement in 1989.

His marriage in 1952 to a Welsh-speaker proved crucial in his development as a writer for he found inspiration in her at a time when he was discovering the literature which was to remain, along with his religious faith, the driving force of his career. At this time, too, he joined Plaid Cymru, to which he remained committed for the rest of his life. The poems in his first book, *Y Gân Gyntaf* (1957), celebrate 'a new Adam' who has fallen in love with the Welsh language, the natural world and his wife all at the same time. They throb with the joys of youth and bristle with breathtaking imagery which spurns common usage and creates a welter of fresh, but sometimes incongruous metaphor. With this book he earned a reputation as an *enfant terrible*, infuriating his elders with his spirited attacks on the sacred cows of the Welsh literary establishment but winning the admiration of most younger poets. His autobiography, published in 2000, is typically entitled *O'r Bedd i'r Crud*.

A dozen more collections of verse followed, notably *Man Gwyn* (1965), written while he was at Laval University in Quebec, *Yr Wyl Ifori* (1967), inspired by a visit to Ghana, and *Allor Wydn* (1971), largely autobiographical and including a long poem dedicated to a young nurse who saved his life when he fell ill during a trip to Mexico City in 1968. After the publication of *Gwlad Llun* in 1976, perhaps in a belated response to complaints that he was writing too much, he announced that he would publish no more verse for ten years. He found it difficult to keep his word but it did not stop him writing. In 1986 there appeared *Hunllef Arthur*, an anti-epic poem about key figures and moments in Welsh history but taking in a variety of topics such as the class war, the institution of marriage, feminism, the brotherhood of man, old age and the love of God. At 21,743 lines it is the second longest poem in Welsh. Few have been able to read it in its entirety but it has some excellent passages; the wags now began saying that Bobi Jones had more books to his name than readers. Undeterred, indefatigable, and always ready to confound his critics by keeping at least one step ahead of them, he continued to publish. His collected poems appeared in three volumes between 1989 and 1995 and a further collection, *Ynghylch Tawelwch*, in 1998. It is possible to make a distinction between the early poetry of Bobi Jones and the later work, pointing to the indelible mark left by his Calvinism on the poems written after 1953 and it was the brazenly Evangelical strand in his thinking which put off many of his more liberal-minded readers but which had a strong appeal among people of the same faith. Joseph P. Clancy translated his *Selected Poems* in 1987.

His three novels are *Nid yw Dŵr yn Plygu* (1958), *Bod yn Wraig* (1960), and *Epistol Serch a Selsig* (1997). Making no concessions to the common reader, these books are difficult even for those familiar with literary theory and are in no whit meant to be popular – a category he despised and for the promoting of which he often took the Welsh Books Council to task. In his view the Welsh reader needed to be fully stretched, for the integrity and vitality of the language depended on it. He regarded those poets who were content to bring out their slim volumes and then fall silent as exemplars of the Welsh inferiority complex, on which he was fond of dilating at every opportunity. His collections of short stories included *Ci wrth y Drws* (1968), *Daw'r Pasg i Bawb* (1969), *Pwy Laddodd Miss Wales?* (1977), *Crio Chwerthin* (1990), and *Dawn Gweddwon* (1992) and are more accessible than his novels but even so they do not make for light reading. In recent years, instead of publishing his work in book-form, he had taken to putting it on his website.

Bobi (Robert Maynard) Jones, writer of the Welsh language, born 20 May 1929, died 22 November 2017.

The Independent (23 November 2017)

HARRI PRITCHARD JONES

Catholic writer and doctor

HARRI PRITCHARD JONES was among the most urbane of Welsh prose-writers, a doctor by profession and, a convert to Roman Catholicism, an Hibernophile and Francophile whose work was influenced by Irish and French writers in both its modernism and its concern for traditional ways of life. Although he wrote exclusively in Welsh, most of his stories and novels are set outside Wales and deal with characters and events far beyond the usual confines of contemporary Welsh literature.

That he wrote in Welsh at all was a piece of good fortune, for he was born in Dudley, Worcestershire, a fact on which he sometimes reflected with wry humour, though his Welsh-speaking parents soon brought him back to Wales and he grew up to speak the language in Menai Bridge and Llangefni in Anglesey.

Welsh meant a great deal to him, not only as the medium for his literary work but also as the language of a small community of Catholics who, mostly under the influence of Saunders Lewis, one of the founders of Plaid Cymru, have made it the language of their religious, intellectual and social life. This connexion made him something of a *rara avis* in the republic of Welsh letters but also gave him a perspective that helped him to write perceptively about his own country and its people, seeing them, as Lewis had taught, as part of an European civilization unfettered by the influence of English thought and customs. He was the only Welshman of my acquaintance who habitually read *The Irish Times*, *The Tablet*, *Le Monde* and *The New York Review of Books* as well as the Welsh-language periodical press.

As a layman in the Catholic Church, to which he turned from agnosticism in 1958, Jones was a close associate of the Welsh-speaking Archbishop Daniel Mullins and other luminaries. A shadow was cast over his many years of loyal service to the Church when, in 2000, the Archbishop of Cardiff, John Aloysius Ward, was involved in controversy over the appointment of a paedophile priest which eventually led to Ward's resignation. The cleric had been accused but acquitted of indecent assault on boys, but instead of sending him for specialist psychiatric assessment, Ward asked Jones to interview him, after which he was cleared as fit for the priesthood. The subsequent revelation that the priest was an active paedophile caused the doctor great heartache.

Although a fairly devout Catholic, Jones found himself unable to accept all the Vatican's teachings, especially those regarding birth control and the role of women in the Church. He was ecumenical in his attitude to other faiths and attempted to reconcile some of his beliefs with those of Welsh Nonconformity, notably in *Cyffes Pabydd wrth ei Ewyllys* (1996), a collection of essays which are little more than short homilies about ethical problems posed by life and death.

The English writer whose influence he was readiest to acknowledge was Graham Greene, author of *The Power and the Glory*, but he was more deeply engaged with the work of the patrician, right-wing, medievalist Saunders Lewis, translating his plays for television and editing an anthology of his writings, *Saunders Lewis: a Presentation of his Work* (1990). When ribbed by his more liberal friends about his admiration for a writer whom many consider the arch-reactionary of modern Wales, he would always point to Lewis's very real achievement as a dramatist and literary critic, while conceding that as a politician he had been an utter failure.

After attending Llangefni Grammar School, Jones studied medicine at Trinity College, Dublin, where he became deeply immersed in Irish culture and a friend of many well-known personalities such as the broadcaster Seán Mac Réamoinn, the composer Seán Ó Riada, the scholar Proinsias Mac Cana and the writer Máirtín Ó Cadhain. Dublin, where he spent ten years, became a second home to him and many of his stories and novels are set in Ireland. But the time he spent as a locum on the Aran Islands proved crucial to his development and vision as a writer. It was there, while serving a community that had changed little since Synge's day, he began writing the stories published in his first book, *Troeon* (1966), some of which are set on Inis Mór and others in Paris, where he was a regular visitor. By that year he had found employment in the mental hospital at Hensol, near Pontyclun, just outside Cardiff, and later worked with patients at the hospital in Whitchurch, a northern suburb of the city.

His first novel, *Dychwelyd* (1972), also set in Dublin, both in intellectual circles and in the seedier working-class parts of the city, won an Arts Council prize in the year of its publication. Two more collections of stories confirmed his reputation as a prose-writer of consummate skill and power: *Pobl* (1978) and *Ar y Cyrion* (1994), the first of which was translated as *Corner People* (1991) and in both of which the delicate evocation of place, whether the backstreets of Cardiff or the boulevards of Paris, is matched by masterly analysis of human motives and behaviour. Two of his stories appear in English translation in the *Penguin Book of Welsh Short Stories*.

His novel *Ysglyfaeth* (1987), of which a film was made for television, is a love-story set in Wales and against the background of conflict in Northern Ireland, while *Bod yn Rhydd* (1992) deals with social deprivation and the plight of ethnic minorities in Cardiff, specifically with the experiences of a black prisoner from the dockland area of Butetown and those of his white wife who works in a hospital for the mentally handicapped. Jones's interest in psychiatry also prompted him to write a monograph on Sigmund Freud in the series *Y Meddwl Modern* (1982).

Jones was a fervent believer in trying to bring the literature of his country into contact with European modernism by translation from and into Welsh. Among the writers whose work he translated was Albert Camus, whose story *'Les Muets'* appeared in the anthology *Storïau Tramor* which he edited in 1974. The story took its place with work by, among others, Kafka, Maupassant, Babel, Unamuno, Verga, Strindberg, O'Flaherty and Joyce, the last-named represented by a Welsh version of his masterpiece, 'The Dead'. Jones might have done much more good work of this kind, but by his own admission he was easily enticed from his desk by invitations to sit on committees, write journalism, and appear on radio and television as one of the comparatively few Welsh-speakers able to speak for his Church. He was Joint Chairman of the Welsh Academy, the national association of writers in Wales, and was usually to be found at its meetings and conferences, after which he would hold court in inimitable style and well into the small hours.

An early member of *Cymdeithas yr Iaith Gymraeg*, founded in 1962 with the aim of winning official status for Welsh, he took part in many of the militant campaigns of the 1970s and, in 1973, was gaoled for 30 days for refusing to pay his television licence as part of the call for the creation of a fourth channel broadcasting in Welsh. In the cells of Cardiff gaol he saw at first hand how abominably inmates were treated and was disconcerted to find himself being given more sympathetic treatment by warders who recognized him as a doctor who was frequently called to the rougher parts of the city. One of his most impassioned lectures, in which he made a plea for more compassionate sentences, was given to a conference of magistrates in 1980.

A bon viveur and the most companionable of men, Harri Pritchard Jones was fond of good food and red wine in generous helpings. During a visit to Georgia and Abkhazia in 1975 he impressed our hosts, writers renowned for their gargantuan appetites, by matching them glass by glass, bottle by bottle, without much sign of being worse for wear. He delighted in the resemblance between *gvin*, the Georgian word for wine, and *gwin*, its Welsh equivalent.

At their home in Whitchurch he and his wife Lenna, a radio producer, kept open house for friends and visitors to the city who were always encouraged to talk about the latest news and gossip in the cultural and political life of Wales and Ireland. Welsh was the language of their home and their children speak it in their professional lives: one of their sons, Guto Harri, is often seen on the television news from London and in feature programmes broadcast by BBC Cymru.

Harri Pritchard Jones, doctor and writer: born Dudley, in what was then Worcestershire, 10 March 1933; married 1965 Lenna Harries (two sons, one daughter); died Cardiff, 11 March 2015.

RHIANNON DAVIES JONES

Writer who addressed contemporary themes in her historical novels

RHIANNON DAVIES JONES was a novelist's novelist whose graceful prose-style was described by one eminent critic as 'fine as gossamer'. Writing in a rich Welsh, both erudite and colloquial, she was able to convey the essence of character and plot with an ease that was much admired by other writers.

There had been historical novels in the language before she began writing in the 1950s but with the appearance of her short novel, *Fy Hen Lyfr Cownt* (1961), the genre gathered a momentum that it has maintained to the present day.

This was a fictional diary of the late eighteenth-/early nineteenth-century hymn-writer and mystic Ann Griffiths (*née* Thomas) whose words were later set to the famous hymn-tune 'Cwm Rhondda'. It won the Prose Medal at the National Eisteddfod and has been held in high esteem ever since. The book succeeds remarkably well in expressing the everyday concerns of a simple countrywoman and her intense spiritual life at a time of religious fervour in Wales.

She used the diary form again in the novel *Lleian Llan Llŷr* (1965), an exploration of the joys and anguish of the cloistered religious life for which she was awarded the Prose Medal for a second time. She then found her stride with *Llys Aberffraw* (1977), which is related by Angharad, the illegitimate daughter of one of Prince Owain Gwynedd's daughters.

It was prompted by the unhappy events of summer 1969, especially the investiture of the Queen's eldest son as 'Prince of Wales' and the deaths of two young activists at Abergele, killed by their own explosives shortly before the ceremony.

This dimension of the novel, sensitively drawn and eloquently expressed, made it one of the most popular books in the troubled period of the 1960s.

Her next novel, *Eryr Pengwern* (1981), is set in seventh-century Powys at a site traditionally located near Shrewsbury, and is based on the Heledd Saga, one of the greatest expressions of grief and longing in the Welsh language. It was written during the campaign for a Welsh-language television channel and concludes on an optimistic note.

She returned to the journal form in *Dyddiadur Mari Gwyn* (1985) which deals with the Catholic recusant Robert Gwyn, the most prolific Welsh writer of the Elizabethan age, who is chiefly remembered as the putative author of a book partly printed in a cave on the Little Orme, near Llandudno.

There followed a trilogy of novels on an even more ambitious scale: *Cribau Eryri* (1987), *Barrug y Bore* (1989) and *Adar Drycin* (1993). All three are set in the Age of the Princes – Llywelyn the Great, his son Dafydd, and Llywelyn the Last, who was killed by Anglo-Norman forces at Cilmeri, near Builth, in 1282. Her description of medieval battle is particularly vivid but it is the effect of violence on ordinary lives that is most important for her. Her princes and warriors are not cardboard cut-outs but real people caught up in events that test and often overwhelm them.

Her last book was *Cydio mewn Cwilsyn* (2002), the fictitious diary of the daughter of Edmwnd Prys, archdeacon of Meirionnydd and Renaissance scholar. She also published nursery rhymes for children and short stories.

The authenticity of her novels, ten in all, has won for Rhiannon Davies Jones an assured place among Welsh novelists and her impassioned use of historical fact to convey a clear nationalist point of view has commended her to a new generation of readers. Her work can be compared, in Welsh, only with that of the distinguished novelist Marion Eames.

The daughter of a minister, she was born at Llanbedr in the old county of Meirionnydd, brought up in Llanfair near

Harlech and educated at the grammar school in Ruthin and the University College of North Wales, Bangor. After teaching Welsh in Llandudno and Ruthin, she was appointed to a lectureship at the College of Education in Caerleon, and later became a senior lecturer at the Normal College, Bangor.

Rhiannon Davies Jones, novelist: born Llanbedr, Meirionnydd, 3 November 1921; died Holyhead, Ynys Môn, 22 October 2014.

The Independent (28 October 2014)

CERI W. LEWIS

Welsh scholar who stayed true to his native Rhondda

CERI W. LEWIS came late to the field of scholarship but, by dint of his immense industry and intellectual gifts, made an important contribution to Welsh literary criticism, historiography, philology and grammar.

He was born, a collier's son, in Treorci in the Rhondda Valley in 1926, the year of the General Strike when the miners of south Wales held out against the government of Stanley Baldwin for seven months after the Trades Union Council had capitulated to its demands. The hungry years of the 1930s left an indelible mark on him but, unlike many of its talented sons, he saw no reason for moving from the Valley, and lived all his life in his native place.

After leaving Porth Boys' Grammar School, in his day one of the best secondary schools in south Wales, and where he had excelled at Welsh, English and Latin, he became a Bevin Boy – one of the workforce named after the Minister for Labour, Ernest Bevin, who were recruited to work in the coal industry. Lewis, at the age of 18, went to work underground in Cwm-parc, where he narrowly missed being killed by roof falls on several occasions. The experience gave him a robust physique, a calm, almost phlegmatic personality and, in private, a mischievous sense of humour which served him in good stead in later life.

One advantage of working as a Bevin Boy was that he was eligible after four years for a grant to enable him to go to university, and this he did in 1948, enrolling at University College, Cardiff, to read Welsh, History and English. He was among the best-read of all undergraduates in his year, having immersed himself in books on Welsh grammar, prosody and literature by such eminent scholars as John Morris Jones, Thomas Parry and Henry Lewis while attending the boys' club in Treorci. He had also read an English translation of *Das Kapital* while still in the sixth form.

The man who had the greatest influence on him at Cardiff was Griffith John Williams, the Professor of Welsh, whom he took as his Gamaliel and who considered him one of the most outstanding students ever to sit at his feet. After graduating with a First in both Welsh and History, he immediately took up a post as lecturer in both departments; four years later he severed his connection with History. Promoted Senior Lecturer in Welsh in 1965 and Reader in 1973, he was given a personal Chair in 1976 and made Head of Department in 1979.

Among his many contributions to scholarly symposia and journals were his long article on the history of the Welsh Church in *Llên Cymru* (1957), on the Treaty of Woodstock signed by Llywelyn the Great and the English king in 1247 in *The Welsh History Review* (1964), and on the Bardic Order in *A Guide to Welsh Literature* (1976). Even more important are the two chapters he contributed to the *Glamorgan County History* (1971, 1974) and substantial chapters on the Welsh language in *The Cardiff Region* (1960), a survey published in 1960 on the occasion of the British Association's visit to Cardiff.

Another of his special interests was Iolo Morganwg, the wayward genius who in 1792 invented the Gorsedd of Bards of the Isle of Britain whose arcane rituals still add colour to the annual ceremonies of the National Eisteddfod. Iolo's brilliant forgeries had been exposed in 1926 by Lewis's old professor, Griffith John Williams, and he added a great deal of research into his life and work.

Ceri Lewis was immensely proud of his connections with the Rhondda and wrote extensively about its Welsh-language traditions before the discovery of coal, most notably in *Rhondda Past and Future* (1975). His own Welsh was untypical of the Valley in that it was polished, highly literary and showed little trace of a local accent, though he could speak a more demotic form of the language when the occasion required it, as when he appeared on television on behalf of the passengers' group trying to improve the train service between Cardiff and the Rhondda.

He combined his scholarly activity with assiduous service on most of the University's committees responsible for the teaching of the Welsh language and its literature. These included the Board of Celtic Studies, of which he was a member for more than 40 years, the Editorial Board of *Geiriadur Prifysgol Cymru* (the University of Wales Dictionary), and the University of Wales Press Board. He edited *Llên Cymru*, one of the most prestigious of Welsh scholarly journals, for ten years.

Many honours came his way. He was elected Fellow of the Society of Antiquaries and of the Royal Historical Society early in his career. In 1990 he was awarded the Leverhulme Emeritus Fellowship and in 1995 he was appointed O'Donnell Lecturer at the University of Wales.

By then, however, he was no longer employed as Professor of Welsh at Cardiff. When in 1987 the University College nearly went into bankruptcy, there were some who pressed for the closing of the Welsh Department as a way of saving money and they nearly had their way. But Lewis argued staunchly in favour of sparing his department from the impending cuts, not least because he believed passionately that Welsh should be taught in the capital city of Wales. His efforts bore fruit, but only at great cost to himself: the department survived but his own post was abolished in April 1987.

He nevertheless continued, unpaid and without even an office on campus, to supervise the work of his students and colleagues until the academic year came to an end in the following June. Shortly before his departure, he received the unusual compliment of a letter signed by all students in the

Welsh Department in which they thanked him for his labours on their behalf. It was to be several years before Welsh studies at Cardiff recovered from the shock of losing Ceri W. Lewis.

Ceri Williams Lewis, scholar: born Treorci, Glamorgan, 31 August 1926; Lecturer, Senior Lecturer, Reader and Professor of Welsh, University College, Cardiff, 1957–87, and Emeritus; married 1956 Sarah (Sali) Phillips (one son); died Edinburgh, 29 April 2016.

DAVID LYN

Actor and pioneer of radical theatre

DAVID LYN BELONGED to a generation of gifted actors who came to prominence in the late 1960s as the call for a national theatre for Wales once more made its way to the top of the agenda. He put a good deal of his energies into theatre politics, perhaps at the expense of his acting abilities, and was for a while a leading figure in what seemed a serious bid to provide high-quality, indigenous theatre in a land virtually starved of it.

Wales, it has been said, is the only country in the world to have had television in its own language before it had professional theatre, and the truth of that bleak statement is nowhere more evident than in the history of several attempts to found a National Theatre, often against overwhelming odds. It is a gloomy tale of insufficient funding and muddled thinking on the part of public bodies, a lack of suitable buildings, a full complement of inflated artistic egos, the clash of political factions whose typical stance was at one another's throats and the indifference of a public which, until recent times, had little experience of watching plays on the professional stage.

David Lyn came close to success in 1966 when he took the lead in creating a new theatre company known as Theatr yr Ymylon. Although its title made clear it was a 'fringe theatre', the founder's declared intention from the start was that it should grow into a company which had a realistic claim to being considered a 'national' theatre. Alas, the venture lasted only until 1976 when, among much recrimination, Lyn resigned as Artistic Director.

He was an unlikely protagonist in the skirmishes and

pitched battles of Welsh theatre, not least on account of his gentle manner and lack of personal ambition. Born at Porth in the Rhondda Valley into an English-speaking home, but brought up on a smallholding in Cynwil Elfed in Carmarthenshire, he shared the poverty that was all around him. But his mother insisted that he go to the local grammar school, and from there he proceeded to Trinity College, Carmarthen, to train as a teacher.

By the sheerest good fortune he enrolled on a weekend Drama course, at which his acting talents were spotted by the tutor, a lecturer in the Drama Department at the Royal College of Music, and she encouraged him to move to London. After two years at the RCM, where Rose Bruford was Head of Drama, he decided he was ready to earn a living as an actor, much against his parents' wishes but now smitten with the freedom and excitement of working in the theatre.

He made his debut not in the mainstream commercial theatre then dominated by Olivier, Gielgud, Schofield and Redgrave, but in experimental theatre clubs and such avant-garde places as the Watergate, where the actors sometimes improvised and directors took risks in productions that were eventually to become fertile ground for new talent under the supervision of Joan Littlewood, George Devine and others.

After 15 years on the London stage, and with his second wife and five children to support, he decided he had learned enough to put himself to the test back home in Wales. At the time he had just completed a tour of Ireland in *The Caretaker* with the Welsh Theatre Company, which had been founded in 1965. This was the company which, two years later, was to cause bitter controversy and become embroiled in a legal inquiry after it had usurped the title 'Welsh National Theatre' against the wishes of some of its directors, including the eminent writer Emyr Humphreys. Lyn had also been engaged for a season as leading man at the Belgrade Theatre in

Coventry, and so he thought his career was putting on some muscle. It was, nevertheless, a brave even foolhardy move, given the fraught state of theatre in Wales.

It was at this point that a script was sent to him by Cwmni Theatr Cymru, the Welsh-language counterpart of the Welsh Theatre Company, of a play by Gwenlyn Parry, the foremost young Welsh dramatist of the day. The play was *Saer Doliau*, an enigmatic fable in the style of the French playwrights of the Absurd, at the end of which, famously, a telephone rings out across an empty stage, with the audience left to ponder whether it may be a call from the Gaffer/God.

David Lyn's forays into theatre in Wales had hitherto been typically dismal: he had appeared in television productions of Richard Llewellyn's *How Green Was My Valley* and Francis Brett Young's *The House Under the Water*, to no great acclaim. But the invitation from Wilbert Lloyd Roberts, the Artistic Director of Cwmni Theatr Cymru, was to be the making of him. He quickly brushed up his Welsh to a standard which enabled him to master the long speeches and subtly existential language of the play. The production was a resounding success and toured Wales for more than a year.

What had started as a cautious investigation into the state of theatre in Wales developed, largely in response to the blandishments of Ray Smith, Plaid Cymru activist and actor, into a full-time commitment: Welsh theatre, Lyn concluded, had to be his first and only interest. One of the few actors at the time who were bold enough to burn their boats in this way, he became an inspirational figure for younger men and women who had been looking for just this kind of lead.

His lack of fluent Welsh caused him no difficulty because his fellow-actors were always ready to make allowances at rehearsals; it was only when he started to become involved in theatre politics that he felt the strain, notably through the malign influence of Equity, which was wont to condone conditions in Wales which it would not tolerate in England.

He was also appalled by attitudes at the Welsh Arts Council where some older Drama Committee members treasured fond memories of Sybil Thorndike at Tonypandy and Lewis Casson in Dowlais, entertaining the forlorn hope that Welsh actors of international status could somehow be enticed to return to their homeland. He was equally impatient with the Welsh Theatre Company under Warren Jenkins, whose policy was to employ English and expatriate Welsh actors whose career prospects lay chiefly in England but who were prepared to work in Wales when otherwise they would have been 'resting'.

It was time to make a move. The first initiative Lyn took was to form a Welsh Actors' Society. 'Whenever it spoke,' he wrote in an essay in the symposium *Artists in Wales* in 1977, 'it almost frightened itself to death. It eventually made itself articulate on some important union matters after it had converted itself into the Welsh Committee of Equity. On theatre policy it was quite without courage and in the habit of congratulating the establishment it had set out to criticise.'

The next step was to create a new theatre company in an attempt to give Welsh actors confidence to shake off English influences and to build something new and essentially Welsh. The company, Theatr yr Ymylon, was based in Bangor. The public's response was enthusiastic and soon, perhaps too soon, there was talk that it would develop into the national theatre which had proved a chimera for so long. But the St David's Theatre Trust, an umbrella group bringing together a number of disparate interests under the aegis of the Arts Council, foundered amid arguments over what exactly constituted a national theatre and, as an alternative, a network of arts centres and workshops devoted to community-based activity grew in its place.

David Lyn struggled on, convinced there was a role for the experimental in Welsh theatre in both Welsh and

English. But the administrative burden was heavy and, with inadequate resources at his disposal, he found the going hard. The main problems arose from having to satisfy the Arts Council as well as the managers of the dozen or so theatres at which the company performed. 'Eventually,' Lyn wrote, 'I began to torture myself with the suspicion that the company's cautious interpretation of its policy was a symptom of low moral conviction, that the eruption of radical feeling which had originally created the company had lost its impetus and that it was becoming extremely difficult for me to influence its progress towards new and adventurous projects. I was obliged to examine my relationship to the company and concluded that my aspirations were no longer represented there.'

One of the company's last productions was Peter Gill's *Small Change* which toured Wales in 1977, by which time Lyn had severed his connection with it. Thereafter he resumed his career as a television actor, notably in an adaptation of Jack Jones's novel, *Off to Philadelphia in the Morning*, which was based on the life of the composer Joseph Parry. He also continued to produce plays for Theatr Powys, including a couple more by Gwenlyn Parry and *Esther* by Saunders Lewis, and with two of his children, Tim and Hannah, he was involved in producing plays for the stage and television.

In his last years he put much effort into renovating old houses and filling them with Welsh oak antique furniture about which he knew a great deal. But he never again came to public notice and his important contribution as a radical pioneer with a progressive and independent mind was largely overlooked. He was not bitter but was given to warning friends of the perils of trying to create modern theatre in Wales. It was not until 2004 that a Welsh National Theatre was formed and he played no part in it, but if ever there is a gallery of portraits in the new building, it will certainly have a place for one of David Lyn.

David Lyn Jenkins (David Lyn), actor and theatre director: born Porth, Rhondda, Glamorgan, 1927; married Faith Owen (marriage dissolved, one son), secondly 1965 Sally Pepper, deceased (one son, three daughters); Artistic Director, Theatr yr Ymylon, 1966–77; died Cardiff, 4 August 2012.

The Independent (17 October 2012)

ELAINE MORGAN

Author whose most celebrated works
expounded the Aquatic Ape Theory of evolution

ELAINE MORGAN, AUTHOR of the international bestseller *The Descent of Woman*, a feminist view of evolution, enjoyed a brief celebrity shortly after its publication in 1972, mainly on account of her brilliantly argued thesis that humans had their origins in the sea and that women are not biologically or socially inferior to men. But she earned a living by writing scripts, mainly serials and documentary dramas, for television – work for which she never received her full meed of praise.

Perhaps her best-known adaptation was that of Vera Brittain's *Testament of Youth* (1980), which reflected her own feelings about war and women's struggle for education, but she also wrote many documentaries which were widely admired for the skills she brought to the small screen. They include treatments of Anne Frank, Madame Curie and, to great acclaim in her native Wales, *The Life and Times of David Lloyd George*, starring Philip Madoc as the eponymous statesman, and a television version of Richard Llewellyn's novel, *How Green Was My Valley*.

Elaine was born in 1920 at Hopkinstown, a mining village at the lower end of the Rhondda Valley and now part of the town of Pontypridd. Her father was a colliery pumpsman who, in the locust years of the 1920s, was often unemployed. From the widespread poverty and industrial strife of the period she learned the Socialism to which she would remain committed for the rest of her life.

After winning an Exhibition to Oxford in 1939, she read English at Lady Margaret Hall, but was so disheartened by having to write critically about literature that she put off all thought of being a writer for more than a decade. Her time as an undergraduate was largely spent debating working-class conditions of which she had first-hand experience. In 1942 she succeeded Anthony Crosland and Roy Jenkins as Chair of the Oxford University Democratic Socialist Club.

At her father's death towards the end of her first term, her mother insisted that she stay on at Oxford, devising ways of earning enough money to keep her there. In her autobiographical play, *A Matter of Degree*, Morgan explored the tensions felt by a working-class student at Oxford. Of her own dilemma she later commented, 'I never felt much of a conflict as to whether I should remain with my own class and keep their outlook in life or identify with the other lot. I always liked the Welsh end more.'

She took a job as a lecturer with the Workers' Educational Association and then, in 1945, settled in Mountain Ash in the Cynon Valley with her husband, Morien Morgan. He taught French at the Boys' Grammar School in Pontypridd where, among us sixth-formers, he cut a dashing figure for having fought in defence of the Spanish Republic. The couple were often to be seen on CND marches and Elaine once shared a platform in Cardiff with Bertrand Russell.

Her formidable intellectual gifts were displayed in all that she wrote. In *The Descent of Woman* she took on not only the Book of Genesis but also anthropologists as diverse as Darwin, Robert Ardrey, Konrad Lorenz and Desmond Morris, reserving her most closely argued strictures for Freud, whom she saw as a major barrier to women's emancipation.

The book had its source in a controversial thesis propounded in 1960 by Alister Hardy, Professor of Marine Biology at Oxford, that many of the characteristics differentiating humans from other primates date from a prehistoric period of aquatic adaptation. Feminists welcomed its emphasis on the role and needs of females, as a challenge to older theories leaning towards a notion of 'man the hunter', but some male professional scientists were scathing about it.

After the book's success (it was translated into 25 languages) Elaine Morgan went on to write three more in which she posited new and thought-provoking theories of human evolution: *The Aquatic Ape* (1982), *The Scars of Evolution* (1990) and *The Descent of the Child* (1994). All three are written in an accessible style, plain but elegant, and address women readers in the main.

Hardy's theory – based on the observation that the subcutaneous fat of humans more closely resembles that of sea mammals than of grassland primates – was derided and largely ignored until the appearance of Morgan's books. Then, in 1995, Professor Phillip Tobias, one of the most eminent proponents of the hypothesis that man had originated on the savannah of Africa, announced in a public lecture that it was mistaken.

Since then the Aquatic Ape, or Riparian, theory as formulated by Hardy and elaborated by Morgan has been given a good deal of favourable publicity, notably in *New Scientist*, *The Observer* and the BBC *Wildlife Magazine*, though a film on the subject made by the BBC Natural History Unit for the Discovery Channel has never been seen in Britain.

Morgan's book *Falling Apart* (1976) is an equally original and indignant study of the rise and decline of urban civilisation from several viewpoints – biological, sociological, psychological, political, economic and historical, but always from the angle of an outsider rather than a city-dweller. Her main concern was to find 'cleaner and greener' alternatives to urban civilisation and many of her insights were derived from living in one of the most polluted post-industrial valleys of south Wales.

Among her arguments were that urbanisation is basically the same under capitalism and communism; that market forces are now beginning to be inimical to the growth of cities; that the great metropolitan centres are no longer the prime generators of wealth but are moving into a parasitical stage; and that the solution to the cities' problems will have to come from outside because city-dwellers are no longer capable of addressing them.

In between writing her four books on evolutionary theory, Elaine lived on her income from television. Her first plays had been for the stage, notably *The Waiting Room* (1958), which had a cast composed entirely of women, but none of them was a hit. Among her first successes on the small screen were three consecutive episodes of *Inspector Maigret*, followed by a dozen of *Dr Finlay's Casebook*, for which, there being so few novels by A.J. Cronin on which to base the series, she had to devise the storylines herself. 'The marvellous thing about Finlay,' she said, 'was that you could say anything and people were not offended: I dealt with syphilis in one and euthanasia in another.'

This last remark was typical of her forthright, but always genial manner, and her willingness to explore in her writing, from a rigorously feminist point of view, themes which provided her with opportunities of challenging received opinion.

She was made a member of the Linnean Society in 2008, was awarded an OBE in 2009 and published her autobiography, *Knock 'Em Cold, Kid*, in 2012.

Elaine Neville Floyd, television scriptwriter and writer on evolutionary theory: born 7 November 1920, Hopkinstown, Pontypridd, Glamorgan; married 1945 Morien Morgan (deceased; three sons, one deceased); died 12 July 2013.

The Independent (14 August 2013)

MOC MORGAN

Champion angler who took President Jimmy Carter fishing

As FISHERMEN'S TALES go, it was perhaps the tallest of them all even by Welsh standards, the one about a Cardiganshire angler taking the President of the United States out in a boat for a spot of fly-fishing. But it was true.

Jimmy Carter, a keen fisherman, was on holiday in west Wales in 1986 when he happened to hear about the prowess of a Tregaron teacher with rod and line and asked to meet him. The two men got on so well that a friendship was struck up between them and they spent whole afternoons in each other's company.

The President returned to Cardiganshire on several subsequent occasions. It is not known how many trout they caught in the chilly waters of Llyn Clywedog and the many streams that feed into it in the uplands of mid Wales. But the President was delighted with his visits, praising the people he met and the natural beauty of the area. 'I've visited more than a hundred countries,' he told a local reporter, 'but none as beautiful as Wales.'

Moc Morgan took it all in his stride, never swanking about his famous friend and always loth to tell journalists what the two anglers had talked about as they tied their flies and cast their lines. Years later he wrote about the encounter with his customary sangfroid in his autobiography, *Byd Moc* (2013).

Although he had travelled widely to take part in angling competitions and bring home trophies from countries around the world, Morgan John Morgan was very much a man of his own square mile. He was born in 1919 at Doldre, a small community near Tregaron, where almost every man was an angler. He was barely able to walk when he was given his own tackle, and grew up in a community where fishing was the common pursuit.

He trained as a teacher and taught at primary schools in the county, latterly as a headmaster in Lampeter. It is said that he would nip out of school during the midday break and go down to the Teifi to cast a few flies. He began every season fishing at Pont Llanio on the very first day of the season. There was something joyous in his zeal for the riparian pastime and its rituals.

Coming close to Izaac Walton's ideal of 'the compleat angler', he was well-read in the literature of angling and published several books about aspects of the sport. He was also a regular columnist with the *Western Mail*, his last piece appearing the day after his death. 'The best fishing is to be found in print and angling has the best literature of all sports,' he wrote with typical panache. Seeing him gently return a fine fish to the water from which he had just hauled it, reminded me of the consummate countryman Mr Crabtree sharing his river lore with young Peter in the strip cartoon of the old *Daily Mirror*.

I met Moc Morgan once in the green room of a television studio where we chatted about *coch-y-bonddu*, the name of a popular fly which is thought to be derived from the Welsh. He was always eager to share his expertise with those who sought it and was a regular broadcaster in both Welsh and English.

One of his great legacies to fishing was in promoting the sport among young people as secretary of the Welsh Salmon and Trout Angling Association. As the group's secretary he introduced competitions among the home nations for under-16s, women and the disabled.

In a 2012 documentary for the Fieldsports Channel he spoke of how he enjoyed the solitude of the riverbank where, he said, he felt alone but never lonely. 'The sport of fishing has the tranquillity of spirit which many are seeking,' he wrote, paraphrasing Walton.

His passion was passed down to his son Hywel, who is a fishing instructor and a World and European Casting champion, and to his granddaughters who are also expert anglers.

Morgan (Moc) John Morgan, angler: born near Tregaron, Cardiganshire, 1919; married first Meirion (deceased; one son, one daughter), secondly Julia; died Aberystwyth, Ceredigion, 25 May 2015.

The Independent (19 August 2015)

RHODRI MORGAN

First Minister of Wales who stayed close to his people

RHODRI MORGAN WAS the charismatic leader of Labour in Wales from 2000 to 2009 and First Minister at the National Assembly at a time when the fledgling body, after a rocky start, needed stability and credibility. He had been a devolutionist since his student days and, always ready with a colourful phrase, when asked by Jeremy Paxman whether he could see himself in the top job he replied, 'Do one-legged ducks swim in circles?' Paxman, bemused, could only respond with 'Is that Welsh for yes?' As First Minister Morgan proved himself a consummate politician and a popular, if sometimes controversial, figure in the public life of Wales.

With his wife Julie Morgan (*née* Edwards), MP for Cardiff North from 1997 to 2010 and now an Assembly Member, whom he married in 1967, he formed one of the most attractive couples on the Welsh political scene. They made their home at Michaelston-le-Pit, a village near Wenvoe in the Vale of Glamorgan, and had a son and two daughters. Both were very proud of their roots in Cardiff and if Rhodri sometimes assumed an overly proletarian persona that belied his upbringing in a comfortable, cultured home in Radyr on the city's northern outskirts, it was indulged by his mainly working-class constituents, who took him to their hearts as one of their own, for he had a total lack of pretension and deep democratic instincts. He had a personal following that most politicians can only envy.

Hywel Rhodri Morgan was born in Cardiff on 29 September 1939, the younger son of T.J. Morgan and his wife Huana. His left-leaning father later became Registrar of the University of Wales and, in 1961, Professor of Welsh at the University College of Swansea. After leaving Whitchurch Grammar School in his native city he went up to St John's College, Oxford, where he read Philosophy, Politics and Economics (PPE), and thence to Harvard University where he took a Masters in Government in 1963. His time in America proved crucial in the development of his political views, particularly in his critical thinking about international capital and the role of the banks, and he returned as a member of the Labour Party.

His first job was with the South Wales Area of the Workers' Educational Association from where he moved to the Welsh Office and the Department of Employment, but he was quickly promoted to the post of Industrial Development Officer with South Glamorgan County Council and became Head of the Press and Information Bureau of the European Commission in Wales in 1980.

During his time as the Labour MP for Cardiff West, between 1987 and 2001, he served as Opposition spokesman on Energy (1988–92) and on Welsh Affairs (1992–97), and after the return of a Labour government he took the chairmanship of the Public Administration Select Committee. But his mercurial, idiosyncratic, unbiddable personality did not endear him to Tony Blair and the more pinstripe elements of New Labour, to say nothing of his Afro-style hair, dodgy dress sense and a penchant for witty word-play and his lack of deference towards the party's grandees.

There was also the somewhat disorganized domestic condition of Lower House in Michaelston-le-Pit. It was said that Tony Blair, on an overnight stay, raised an eyebrow at what he saw as the state of the Morgan household, in particular when the family dog was allowed to lick the breakfast dishes. Matters were not helped when Julie's mother addressed him as Mr Lionel Blair. In a famous phrase, Morgan resolved to put 'clear red water' between

Labour in Wales and the Blair government, thus beginning a stand-off between the National Assembly and the Labour Party that continues to this day.

Needless to say, Rhodri was not Tony Blair's choice as First Minister at the National Assembly and had to wait for Ron Davies, 'the father of Welsh devolution', and the less effective Alun Michael to quit the office before he could come into his own. He made a great success of it, to such an extent that the Welsh embraced devolved government as the natural order of things. Perhaps the most memorable phase came after 2007 when his party went into coalition with Plaid Cymru, thus combining the two radical traditions of modern Welsh politics with pleasing results. He stepped down soon afterwards, having undergone heart surgery.

In retirement he lived quietly at Lower House, spending his time gardening, wood-carving and long-distance running. He had an encyclopaedic knowledge of rugby and his favourite place was Mwnt in Ceredigion where the family spent every holiday in a static caravan. He had already written affectionately of his home city in a lively booklet, *Cardiff: Half and Half a Capital*, in which he argued with typical wit and sensitivity about what needed to be done before it could be considered a proper capital, and in which the devolutionist he had always been came to the fore. He also wrote a lively column for the *Western Mail* that reflected his lifelong interest in Welsh, British, European and American politics.

The genuine affection and respect in which Rhodri was held was evident on the day his death was announced when members of all parties stood for a minute's silence in the milling area of the National Assembly, electioneering was postponed and flags on the building flew at half-mast. He died suddenly while cycling in the lanes near his home.

Rhodri Morgan leaves his wife Julie, their three children and his brother Prys, who is Emeritus Professor of History at Swansea University.

Rhodri Morgan, politician: born Cardiff, 29 September 1939; married 1967 Julie Edwards (one son, two daughters); died 17 May 2017.

JAMES NICHOLAS

Archdruid of Wales and poet of rare sensibility and high learning

THE ASSEMBLY OF Bards of the Isle of Britain (to render *Gorsedd Beirdd Ynys Prydain* in English) is perhaps the most picturesque of all Welsh institutions. Every August, as part of the festivities of the National Eisteddfod, it is at the heart of the literary ceremonies, its members parading in their robes, its officials carrying the regalia and banners that proclaim '*Y gwir yn erbyn y byd*' ('The truth against the world') in an impressive display of neo-druidic ritual and bardic fervour.

The man or woman who presides over this arcane pageantry is the Archdruid, elected from among the serried ranks of the *Gorsedd* and usually a distinguished writer, whether of prose or verse, who has achieved the feat of carrying off one of the major prizes such as the Chair (for verse in the traditional metres), the Crown (for free verse) or the Prose Medal (for a novel, short stories or essays). Although membership is often bestowed on non-literary people who have nevertheless made a contribution to public life in Wales, such as teachers, civil servants and rugby players, the office of Archdruid is invariably reserved for writers, still regarded by the people as natural leaders who are venerated for their command of the Welsh language.

James Nicholas, who served as Archdruid for the statutory period of three years from 1981 to 1984, was well within this illustrious tradition. His eligibility stemmed from the fact that he had won the Chair at the National Eisteddfod of 1969 and, as a bonus point, was known to be a poet of rare sensibility and high learning. He was, moreover, a patriot who was unafraid of speaking his mind from the Logan Stone on events affecting the civilisation of Wales and the wider world, especially those threatening peace and social progress. At home, he lent his support to the law-breaking campaigns of the Welsh Language Society and, further afield, the horrors of apartheid and the plight of the Third World were always prominent on his agenda.

In his deep concern for the underprivileged and exploited, James Nicholas was influenced by the great pacifist poet Waldo Williams (1904–71), with whom he had a close personal friendship and with whom he shared a reverence for the writings of the Russian philosopher, Nikolai Berdyaev. He wrote percipiently about Waldo's mysticism and attraction in later life to Quakerism, delivered a moving funeral address, edited a volume of memorial essays and, in many public lectures, explained the cultural background to some of his finest poems, particularly their roots in the rural, co-operative and radical society in which both had been brought up. His monograph on Waldo in the *Writers of Wales* series is still the best introduction in English to the poet's life and work.

James Nicholas was born in the ancient cathedral town of St Davids in Pembrokeshire in 1928. Once described, with only slight hyperbole, as 'the most important native of St Davids since the patron Saint himself', he remained staunchly attached to the town of his birth and it was out of real affection that local people turned up in their hundreds to take part in the tribute paid to him at the National Eisteddfod held there in 2002. The loudest applause on that heart-warming occasion came from his former pupils and fellow-poets.

He had first begun reading poetry when, as a schoolboy, he spent two years in the harsh regime of a sanatorium. This hospitalization meant that he was 20 before he left St Davids Grammar School in 1948 for the University College of Wales, Aberystwyth, where he took a degree in Mathematics. His first teaching post was at Bala in Meirionnydd, one of the heartlands of *Cerdd Dafod*, as the writing of poetry in the strict metres is known, and there he came into contact with country poets who taught him the refinements of traditional verse which, with his quick mathematical mind, he soon mastered. Some of his poems in this mode are comparable with the work of medieval masters and yet wholly contemporary in their preoccupations and allusions.

But it was not long before the magical landscape of Dyfed, land of the Mabinogion, beckoned him home. He was appointed Head of Mathematics at Pembroke in 1959 and Headmaster of Ysgol y Preseli at Crymych in 1963. In the same year he married a colleague, Hazel Griffiths, who was to become his muse and helpmeet in all the ventures in which he was involved. Many of the finest poems in his two collections, *Olwynion* (1967) and *Cerddi'r Llanw* (1969), are about his love for her and their life together.

They had two daughters, one of whom, Branwen, as a leading member of the Welsh Language Society, has served prison sentences for her part in campaigns for official recognition of Welsh. Her parents were steadfast in their support and never flinched from the consequences of her principled stand against the intransigence of officialdom and the harshness of the courts. Their other daughter, Saran, is a member of the Royal College of Physicians.

James Nicholas was interested in a wide range of subjects. As a staunch member of the Welsh Baptist Union, which he served as President, he was immersed in contemporary theology and philosophy, his mind given to the numinous and existentialist. During his time as headmaster at Crymych he was awarded a Fellowship in the Philosophy Department at the University College, Swansea, under Professor Dewi Z. Phillips and was thus able to pursue his interest in Rush Rhees, friend and disciple of Wittgenstein, both of whom had spent some time in Swansea. He was also steeped in the work of Christian poets such as T.S. Eliot, David Jones and R.S. Thomas, and the Marxist T.E. Nicholas, as well as in music and the visual arts.

From 1975 until his retirement in 1988 James Nicholas

was a member of Her Majesty's Inspectorate of Schools and based in Gwynedd. He once told me that, whereas he had enjoyed being a headmaster because he had direct contact with his pupils, he was unsure of his mandarin role as an inspector and regarded his leaving Ysgol y Preseli with some misgiving. He was nevertheless able to maintain his links with the *Gorsedd*, having been elected to serve as Recorder in 1980, a post to which he returned after his stint as Archdruid in 1984.

He took the *Gorsedd* seriously and brought to both posts a dignity that won him many admirers, even among those cynics who never tire of pointing out that the ceremonies are, in fact, the fruit of the febrile genius of Iolo Morganwg, a Glamorgan stonemason who invented them in 1792. A pillar of common sense and the utmost integrity, James Nicholas was charged as Recorder with responsibility for keeping the names of the prize-winning writers confidential over the ten weeks between submission of the written adjudications and the announcements from the Eisteddfod stage, which he did with unfailing skill. He was a consummate committee man who always managed to get the best out of others and his administrative skills were widely admired.

It was fitting that the title of the lecture he delivered at the College of William and Mary in Williamsburg, Virginia, was 'The Secret of the Bards'. Those London newspapers who were perplexed when Rowan Williams, soon to be installed as Archbishop of Canterbury, was admitted to the Order of the White Robe in 2002, would have done well to get hold of a copy of this magisterial lecture before deciding that the *Gorsedd* was 'a pagan institution'.

A modest, genial, eirenic man not given to self-advertisment or caustic comment on others, James Nicholas was a good listener, though some found his habit of looking up at the ceiling when engaged in conversation, as if for heavenly guidance, a trifle disconcerting. The beatific grin that lit up his features seemed to reflect something of the innocence of a child which, in his poems, shines like a ray of God's amazing grace. To be in his company was to be reminded of the famous lines by his friend Waldo Williams: 'To live, what is it? / Having a great hall between cramped walls. / Being a nation, what is it? / A gift in the depths of the heart. / Patriotism, what's that? / Keeping house in a cloud of witnesses.'

James Nicholas, Archdruid of Wales and poet: born St Davids, Pembrokeshire, 19 March 1928; married 1963 Hazel Griffiths (two daughters); died Bangor, Gwynedd, 29 September 2013.

The Independent (17 October 2013)

GERALLT LLOYD OWEN

Welsh poet and broadcaster whose sonorous verse
mourned the creeping loss of his native culture

ONE OF THE most gifted and influential Welsh poets
of modern times, Gerallt Lloyd Owen was a master of
cynghanedd, an ancient system of sound-chiming within a
line of verse involving the serial repetition of consonants in
precise relationship to the main accents in the line, together
with the use of internal rhyme. It is found in primitive form
in the earliest extant poetry of the sixth century and in rich
complexity in the work of the medieval masters, and is still
used to striking effect in modern Welsh poetry.

Gerallt Lloyd Owen was one such master. His poems are
familiar to most literate Welsh-speakers and are often quoted,
especially those written at the time of the investiture of the
Queen's eldest son as 'Prince of Wales' in 1969. Addressing
Llywelyn ap Gruffudd, the last prince of independent Wales,
he wrote:

> Wylit, wylit, Lywelyn,
> Wylit waed pe gwelit hyn.
> Ein calon gan estron ŵr,
> Ein coron gan goncwerwr,
> A gwerin o ffafrgarwyr
> Llariaidd eu gwên lle'r oedd gwŷr.

(You would weep, weep, Llywelyn, weep blood if you saw this. Our
heart with a foreigner, our crown with a conqueror, and a populace
of favour-seekers, with meek smiles, where once were men.)

There was an outpouring of anti-royalist verse in the
period leading up to the investiture but none captured the

angst and contempt so well as Gerallt Lloyd Owen. He saw through the official bluff that Charles was the true Prince of Wales and satirized the obsequious fawning on the monarchy that sickened many a patriot's heart. His first substantial collection of poems, *Cerddi'r Cywilydd* (1972), contained almost all the verse that challenged the veracity of the event at Caernarfon castle in July 1969 and lashed the servility of those Welsh people who had been hoodwinked into accepting it. The poems, republished as a collection in 1990, remain popular to this day.

A second collection, *Cilmeri* (the name of the spot near Builth where Llywelyn the Last Prince was killed by Anglo-Norman forces in 1282), published in 1991, contained more poems than the first, but they were written on a wider spectrum and not all were in *cynghanedd*; in some, the poet assumes the traditional role of the Welsh poet who celebrates community and serves as soothsayer. But all demonstrate Owen's mastery of his medium and in vivid language that sings and resonates to memorable effect. The collection won the Wales Book of the Year prize in 1992.

He was by now recognized as one of the leading poets in the Welsh language, and had won the Chair at the National Eisteddfod in 1975 and 1982. He had also won fame as an adjudicator in the bardic contests broadcast in the popular series on BBC Radio Cymru, *Talwrn y Beirdd*, in which teams of poets in the strict metres are asked to compose impromptu verses, sometimes on humorous subjects, a unique feature of the literary scene in Wales.

His dry, puckish humour as a broadcaster contrasted with the sadness of his poetry which is suffused with a sense of loss as he contemplates the decline of the rural communities he knew in his youth. The influx of English-speakers who move into the Welsh heartlands, often without realizing the damage they do to the native culture, filled him with a profound despair that found its way into his writing. He edited about a dozen selections from *Talwrn y Beirdd*, and from 1976 to

1983 he co-edited *Barddas,* the magazine of *Cymdeithas Cerdd Dafod*, the magazine devoted to new writing in Welsh.

As related in his book *Fy Nghawl Fy Hun* (1999), Gerallt Lloyd Owen was born and brought up in Y Sarnau, Meirionnydd, into a richly cultured family that set great store on the writing and reading of poetry in the traditional metres. He began writing verse as a schoolboy and was soon regarded by his fellow-poets as one who would one day excel in the writing of verse in the strict metres. His brother Geraint is also an accomplished poet. Gerallt was educated at Bangor Normal College and spent some years as a teacher at Trawsfynydd and Bridgend; in the latter place he was on the staff of Ysgol Glyndŵr, a private Welsh-language school established by the philanthropist Trefor Morgan.

He left teaching in 1971 and shortly afterwards, having failed to establish a comic for children, *Yr Hebog*, set up a publishing imprint, Gwasg Gwynedd, which undertook commercial printing as well as the publishing of Welsh books; it flourished for more than 40 years as one of the most prolific and enterprising firms in Wales but recently ceased trading.

At his request, donations instead of flowers were to be sent to the Yes campaign in the referendum on Scottish independence.

Gerallt Lloyd Owen, poet, editor, publisher and broadcaster: born 6 November 1944, Y Sarnau, Meirionnydd; married 1972 Alwena Jones (marriage dissolved, one son, two daughters), partner to Iola Gregory; died Bangor, Gwynedd, 15 July 2014.

The Independent (11 August 2014)

IAN PARROTT

Modernist composer who drew on the Welsh folk tradition

ONE OF THE most prolific and widely performed British composers of his day, Ian Parrott wrote music for orchestra, chamber ensemble, opera and ballet, including symphonies, concertos, string quartets and song cycles, as well as many choral and vocal works and even theme music for documentary films. He combined his huge creative output with his academic and administrative responsibilities as Gregynog Professor of Music at the University College of Wales, Aberystwyth, where he held the Chair from 1950 to 1983.

In a long and distinguished career he won an array of prestigious prizes. These included the first prize of the Royal Philharmonic Society in 1949 for his *Symphonic Impression: Luxor*, the Shakespeare Prize for his *Solemn Overture: Romeo and Juliet* (1953), the Jasper Rooper Prize for his *String Quartet No. 2* (1983) and the British Music Society Prize for his opera *Once Upon a Time* (1985). He took inordinate delight in all these awards, but none gave him more pleasure than the Harriet Cohen International Musicology Medal in 1966.

He was also the author of a dozen books and hundreds of articles on music and musicians. Some of the books, such as *Pathways to Modern Music* (1947) and *A Guide to Musical Thought* (1949), were written for young people in an accessible style that brought him acclaim as a teacher, while others were more substantial studies of Elgar (1971), Cyril Scott (1992) and Peter Warlock (1994). He also contributed regularly to *The Musical Times* and *Music Review* between 1939 and 1993.

As an Englishman long resident in Wales, Parrott took a keen and practical interest in the musical life of his adopted country and, as Gregynog Professor of Music at Aberystwyth, it was natural that he should write *The Spiritual Pilgrims* (1964), a readable but somewhat unsatisfactory account of music-making at Gregynog Hall, near Newtown in Montgomeryshire, which was the home of Gwendoline and Margaret Davies, the granddaughters of industrialist David Davies of Llandinam, whose wealth had made possible, in addition to a famous private press, a festival of music and poetry that brought eminent artists to Wales during the inter-war years.

The selflessly philanthropic but pathologically reserved sisters relied for their choice of music on Sir Walford Davies, who succeeded Sir Edward Elgar as Master of the King's Musick in 1934, and the festival's conductor was Sir Adrian Boult. After the war Ian Parrott conducted a series of ten festivals for Margaret Davies, the surviving sister, to which he attracted such eminent composers as Arthur Bliss, Edmund Rubbra, Gordon Jacob and Mansel Thomas.

Ian Parrott was born in Streatham, London, in 1916, and brought up in Harrow. Encouraged by his mother, who had studied the piano, the hyper-intelligent lad began composing sonatas while still in short trousers. He was educated as a day-boy at Harrow School and from there went to the Royal College of Music; at New College, Oxford, he graduated in 1937 and was awarded his doctorate in 1940. Between 1937 and 1939 he taught Music at Malvern College, occasionally travelling to Worcester to play the viola in Sir Ivor Atkins's orchestra.

During the war he served with the Royal Signals Corps in Egypt, latterly in the rank of Captain. His burlesque opera *The Sergeant Major's Daughter* had its premiere in Cairo in 1943 and his *Symphonic Prelude: El Alamein* was written in the year following. His symphony *Luxor* was inspired by the renowned temple on the Nile which he visited while on leave from the army; he was deeply impressed by the fact that the building included a Roman temple, a Christian altar and, most recent of all, a Muslim mosque. After demobilization in 1946 he became a lecturer in Music at Birmingham University but stayed there only three years prior to his appointment, at the age of 34, to the Chair of Music at Aberystwyth.

He came to public notice in Wales with his second opera, *The Black Ram* (first performed in its entirety in 1957), a retelling of the story of Siôn Philip, a poor tenant falsely accused of sheep-stealing and duly hanged by order of Herbert Lloyd, the infamous squire of Peterwell, a mansion near Lampeter, in the mid-eighteenth century. Parrott returned to Welsh legend with the concert overture *Seithenyn*, which was commissioned and broadcast by the BBC Welsh Orchestra in 1959 and, five years later, performed by the London Philharmonic Orchestra under Sir Adrian Boult. This tone poem was inspired by the tale of the drunkard Seithenyn, best known to English readers from Thomas Love Peacock's novel *The Misfortunes of Elphin* (1829), whose negligence as keeper of the floodgates leads to the drowning of Gwyddno Garanhir's kingdom, Cantre'r Gwaelod, under the waters of what is today Cardigan Bay.

The local success of these two works prompted him to write *The Lady of Flowers* (1981), a chamber opera in two acts based on the tale of Blodeuwedd in the Mabinogion, the woman who commits adultery and is turned by a wizard into an owl (a bird known in Welsh as 'flower-face'). These were perhaps not his most important works but they represent a brave attempt to write serious music on authentically Welsh themes and drawing on Welsh folk melodies, and were much admired for that reason.

A more cultivated musical taste might prefer such works as Parrott's seascape *Arfordir Ceredigion* (1957) for solo harp, or *Fantasy Sonata* (1979) for clarinet and piano, or *Autumn Landscape* (1983) for oboe and piano, all pieces of chamber music, a form at which he consistently excelled.

Also attractive are his song 'I heard a linnet courting' (1940), the cantata *Jubilate Deo* (1963) and the anthem *Surely the Lord is in this Place* (1974), though from such a vast and varied oeuvre, in which pleasing melody is blended with the intricate rhythms of modernist music, it is difficult to choose.

As Gregynog Professor of Music at Aberystwyth, Ian Parrott played a prominent part in Welsh musical life, notably as a founder member and later Chairman of the Guild for the Promotion of Welsh Music, which since its inception in 1954 has done much to raise standards and create a public awareness of the work of contemporary composers. Under his direction, the Music Department, which had fewer than 20 students when he arrived in 1950, had nearly a hundred by 1980. Among its alumni were the composer William Mathias and the singers Redvers Llewellyn and Kenneth Bowen.

He also served as Vice-President of the Elgar Society and was a keen member of the Peter Warlock Society. Unfortunately, his 'autobiography', with its ungainly title *Parrottcisms* (2003), published by the British Music Society, is a disappointing monograph in that it relies, for the most part, on diary jottings and the dropping of famous names, together with a stream of rather self-satisfied comments on his own life and work, but it has a full bibliography and a selection of his contributions to music journals.

Parrott's reputation might have been even greater among musicologists if he had not dabbled in the paranormal. In 1967 he met Rosemary Brown at Attingham Park, an adult education college in Shropshire. She believed that as a child she had received communications from the composers Liszt, Rachmaninoff and Beethoven, who informed her that when she grew up they would dictate new pieces of music to her. By the time her book *Unfinished Symphonies* was published in 1971, Brown had 'composed' some 400 pieces by dead composers.

Ian Parrott wrote of this phenomenon, 'I don't think there

is any cheating here. As a musician I am quite prepared to say that everything she has produced is stylistically possible.' In 1976, encouraged by a Dutch television crew who were making a programme about Rosemary Brown, he orchestrated a movement from an 'F Minor Symphony' which Brown claimed to have received from Beethoven. Despite his assertion that he was a devout Christian, Parrott – he had joined the Society for Psychical Research in 1951 – was fascinated by extrasensory perception and the possibility of communication with the dead, believing with James Elroy Flecker, that 'our garden goes on for ever, out of the world'.

Horace Ian Parrott, composer: born Streatham, London, 5 March 1916; Gregynog Professor of Music, University College of Wales, Aberystwyth, 1950–83, and Emeritus; married 1940 Elizabeth Cox (deceased 1994; two sons), 1996 Jeanne Peckham (deceased); died Aberystwyth, Ceredigion, 4 September 2012.

The Independent (3 December 2012)

DAVID PARRY-JONES

A well-known voice and face in Welsh broadcasting

DAVID PARRY-JONES WAS one of the most accomplished and versatile broadcasters ever produced by the BBC in Wales, or for that matter, anywhere in the United Kingdom. An all-rounder in a broad spectrum of radio and television programmes, he worked as newsreader, reporter, presenter, interviewer and commentator in news, current affairs, religion, documentaries, education and sport, notably rugby union, a game with which he was closely identified in the public's mind for more than 30 years.

As a documentary-maker he was intent on redressing the traditional stereotypes of Wales – pit-head, male voice choir, sheep – by replacing them with images that reflected more accurately the stunning landscapes and vibrant people he knew and admired. He was incensed by what fly-by-night film-crews visiting from England chose to show of contemporary Wales but was also dismayed by what the Welsh were content to tell the world about themselves.

To local councillors who complained that his promotional film of their town in Monmouthshire showed fine buildings, modern amenities and a breathtakingly beautiful hinterland, instead of the grim remnants of industry and social deprivation with which they were more familiar, he pointed out that a similar film about London would focus not on its dreary urban sprawl but on Buckingham Palace, the West End and the Thames. He often waxed lyrical about the natural beauty of Wales and, a staunch patriot, had special affection for her people, their strengths as well as their shortcomings.

David Parry-Jones was born in 1933 in Pontypridd, a

bustling town at the confluence of the Rhondda and Taff rivers in the heart of industrial Glamorgan. His Welsh-speaking father was from Corwen in north Wales and a minister with the Presbyterian Church of Wales, that is to say with the Calvinistic Methodists, perhaps the most conservative of the Welsh Nonconformist denominations, while his mother was an English-speaking teacher from Monmouthshire.

There was a streak of conservative, even Conservative, piquancy in his own thinking, especially with regard to what he considered the baneful influence of trades unions in the broadcasting industry, and he certainly had none of the proletarian mores usually associated with his rugby-loving compatriots. He was, in short, what Kingsley Amis called 'an up-market media Welshman'.

He was brought up in a home that revered scholastic achievement but was unable to speak more than a few phrases of his father's language. His lack of Welsh irked him and, during his career with BBC Wales, he was often to attribute to it the promotion of colleagues to posts which he thought he could have filled better. Like many sons of the manse, with whom the BBC in Wales abounded until recent times, David Parry-Jones inherited his father's mellifluous voice, albeit in English only, and felt himself at home in both north and south Wales, so that he seemed destined to have a career in an all-Wales context such as broadcasting.

His sense of being Welsh was awoken while a pupil at Hoylake Preparatory School on the Wirral, where he was taunted on account of his accent, and at Birkenhead School. He was greatly relieved when his parents brought him home to Cardiff, where his father had taken up a post as Religious Broadcasts Organiser with the BBC Welsh Home Service, and where in 1945 he started as a pupil at the city's High School. It was there he discovered a keen interest in cricket and rugby.

In 1952 he went up to Merton College, Oxford, to read

Classics, graduating four years later but without distinction. At Merton he was usually to be found in the company of 'hearties' and gave a wide berth to the Dafydd ap Gwilym Society in whose meetings his more earnestly Welsh-speaking contemporaries congregated.

Of his time at Oxford he was to write: 'If asked to analyse the Oxford experience, I would cite the conferring of great confidence in social and business discourse. Never since, despite the company of gifted and able individuals in my professional career, have I encountered quite the bracing climate of ideas that the University afforded. Three or four years beside the Isis wrap you in a thick skin which can weather many of the storms which await the career-minded. It also taught me how to deal with the English – in particular their public school trained middle class – which is an art in itself.'

He enjoyed his two years' national service with the Welch Regiment, during which he attained the lowly rank of second lieutenant and was sent to Cyprus at the height of the EOKA campaign and then to Tobruk in Libya. He became particularly fond of squaddies serving with him in the infantry regiments, admiring them for their practical skills and stoical good humour: for many years after demobilization he attended the curry lunches cooked by Gurkhas in Cardiff's Maindy Barracks, renewing old friendships and talking over old times.

His first jobs as a journalist were with the *Western Mail* and *The Sunday Times*, but it was in broadcasting that Parry-Jones was to make his mark. He had taken part in *Children's Hour* as a twelve year old and had broadcast with actors such as Richard Burton and Siân Phillips. He had also represented his school in the *Top of the Form* series during which he had enjoyed several inspirational conversations with Richard Dimbleby. He now landed a job as a newsreader with the BBC in Cardiff, filling a vacancy left by Michael Aspel, and soon learnt the rudiments of reading to camera. With a good broadcasting voice, impeccable manners, a cool head and the Brylcreemed looks of a Don Bradman, he seemed a natural in front of the microphone and camera.

With the creation of BBC Wales in 1963, David found freelance opportunities galore as studio interviewer, commentator and documentary-maker under the tutelage of the legendary Gethin Stoodley Thomas, and in both radio and television. Throughout the 1970s he was paired with John Darran as co-presenter of *Wales Today*, the evening news programme that was the BBC Wales flagship, and was to be seen regularly introducing *Songs of Praise* from Wales and other popular programmes.

But it was as a rugby commentator that he came into his own. For the next 20 years he covered most international matches and had one of the most familiar grandstand voices in the game, as well known in Wales as Bill McLaren's in Scotland; his trademark sheepskin coat, much mocked by wags like Max Boyce for its luxuriant fleece collar, was almost as famous. Parry-Jones's love of rugby, and his intimate knowledge of its ethos and arcania, were evident in all his commentaries, in which he strove to maintain the elegance and dignity of language which he habitually employed in front of the microphone.

This work began to founder in 1979 when BBC Wales devolved its Welsh-language responsibilities to the newly established BBC Cymru and, three years later, with the advent of S4C (the fourth channel which broadcasts in Welsh), he was told that as front-man of *Wales Today* he was to be replaced by younger men and women. Not daunted, and with the former Glamorgan cricketer Peter Walker, he now set up an independent television company known as Merlin which specialized in making corporate videos; it was later sold to Trilion plc but bought back from the Receivers in 1993.

David Parry-Jones wrote several books about rugby with the players Mervyn Davies and David Watkins, including *Taff's Acre*, a history of Cardiff Arms Park, and *Rugby Remembered*, a pictorial account of the game's development as portrayed over a century and a half by the artists and photographers of *The Illustrated London News*.

The resentment he felt at his treatment by BBC Wales was directed towards 'fat cat administrators in the media hierarchy' and this animus inevitably coloured the account he published in *Action Replay: a Media Memoir* (1993), which otherwise provides a lively insight into broadcasting as a career and a genial account by a consummate professional of what he called 'a lifetime in communication with one's native land'.

He is survived by his long-term partner, the broadcaster Beti George, whose moving account of how she nursed him through the last phase of Alzheimer's disease has been shown on BBC Wales.

David Parry-Jones, broadcaster: born Pontypridd, Glamorgan, 25 September 1933; married Janet Evans (one son, one daughter; marriage dissolved); died Penarth, Vale of Glamorgan, 10 April 2017.

The Daily Telegraph (15 May 2017)

MEIC POVEY

Ground-breaking playwright, screenwriter and actor

MEIC POVEY WAS a multi-talented playwright who managed to combine the writing of soap operas with more substantial work for the Welsh theatre and television. Taken under the wing of Gwenlyn Parry, the eminent Welsh dramatist of the Absurd, and employed in the Drama Department of BBC Cymru at a time when the theatre in Wales was enjoying something of a revival, he was encouraged to hone his talents and write prolifically in his native tongue. Having started as a teenaged stagehand, and especially after the advent of S4C, he became one of the most distinguished names in the Welsh pantheon.

His name was synonymous with the success of *Pobol y Cwm*, the immensely popular soap opera which was launched in 1974 and is still running, one of the longest of its kind anywhere in these islands. The series reflects daily life in a fictitious Welsh-speaking village somewhere in west Wales, neither wholly urban nor rural, where the daily round is sometimes ruffled by winds from the wider world.

Meic Povey, as scriptwriter, introduced more contemporary themes into the plots and a racier tone to the dialogue which became his hallmark. He was able to make entertaining, watchable television not only out of the quiddities of village life but from observation and discussion of more challenging issues such as violence, crime, sexual misconduct, divorce, and the problems associated with drug and alcohol abuse.

The wags were fond of pointing out that everyone in the village seemed to have slept with everyone else in evermore bewildering combinations since Povey had been taken on as one of the regular scriptwriters, which was only a slight exaggeration. Gradually the villagers of Cwm Deri came to be seen in a new light, not as the innocent occupants of a never-never land but as our contemporaries living in a real, imperfect world.

For this challenge Meic Povey was fully equipped. He was born on 27 November 1950 in Nant Gwynant near Beddgelert, now in Gwynedd, and grew up on the Llŷn peninsula, the arm of north Wales pointing towards Ireland. His parents were Griffith Povey, an agricultural worker, and his wife Margaret. He returned regularly to his native patch but the influx of English-speakers into Snowdonia and the subsequent loss of community weighed heavily upon him, as it does upon many creative people, and this concern sometimes surfaces in his plays as dark humour.

From the mid-1970s he was obliged to live in Cardiff, where BBC Cymru is located, and where he took to the attractions the capital offers with what can only be described as alacrity. Although generally concerned with impoverished people living on the periphery of society, in his series *Teulu*, set in Aberaeron on the Cardigan Bay coast, which he co-wrote with Branwen Cennard, he presents a picture of a more glamorous, frivolous side of Welsh life that critics were happy to call 'Dallas by the sea'.

Another success was *Byw Celwydd*, a political drama that imagines a National Assembly run by a rainbow coalition of Nationalists and New Conservatives known as The Democrats, with the Socialists in opposition, in which envy and treachery drive the politicians and adultery is almost a way of life.

For the stage he wrote several hard-hitting plays such as *Hogia Ni*, about soldiers returning from Afghanistan. *Nel*, for which he is best remembered, deals with family tensions to do with the inheritance of land, an older generation attached to traditional ways beset by their more affluent, rootless children for whom such things don't matter much. *Sul y Blodau* was based on the story of police raids and detention without charge of some 50 people with nationalist sympathies as part of the CID's unsuccessful attempt to discover who was behind the burning of holiday homes in Wales.

His autobiography *Nesa Peth i Ddim* (2010) pulls few punches. In it he mentions by name the several women with whom he had affairs, and wrote movingly about the death of his wife Gwenda in 2007. He made a point of asking permission of the women to whom he refers and claimed it was readily given. Even so, the passages describing his liaisons make for painful reading.

He had a second string to his bow as an actor in both Welsh and English. Often cast as the Welsh sidekick of an English detective, as in the hit crime series *Minder* (1982–89), in which he played D.C. Taff Jones to Patrick Malahide's D.S. Chisholm, he was able to convey a sense of the sinister without much effort, especially in good cop/bad cop scenes. In *A Mind to Kill*, which went out in both languages, he shared the credits with Philip Madoc in a similar role.

He died of cancer in Cardiff on 5 December 2017; two of his wife's children by an earlier marriage survive him.

Meic Povey, playwright and actor: born Nant Gwynant, Beddgelert, 27 November 1950; married Gwenda (two children); died Cardiff, 5 December 2017.

The Daily Telegraph (28 December 2017)

GWILYM PRICHARD

Painter of the rocky landscapes of
Snowdonia, Brittany and Pembrokeshire

IF KYFFIN WILLIAMS was the Welsh painter who, at least
in the public view, is most often associated with the dark
landscapes of north Wales, especially its cloud-capped
mountains, deep valleys and wild coastline, Gwilym Prichard
is best remembered for a palette that held more colour and for
a more versatile approach to the visual beauty of Eifionydd,
that sea-girt district on the Llŷn peninsula of north-west
Gwynedd.

His canvases have to do with the play of light on the
lanes, fields, farms, boulders, sheep-tracks, bracken, dry
stone walls, thorn-trees pointing the direction of the wind
and 'the blue remembered hills' of his childhood – literally
blue, that is, for he used rich paint, spontaneous brushwork
and the boldest of colour combinations, so that there is a
Mediterranean quality to his work that Kyffin Williams,
whose range rarely strayed beyond grey-green-black-white,
never attempted.

Although influenced early in his career by the older
painter, who remained a friend, Gwilym Prichard soon
showed he was his own man, striking out in search of new
subjects and fresh ways of painting them. The plasticity of
oils held endless fascination for him and he used them in a
variety of ways, including impasto and sgraffito, as well as in
mixed-media compositions of collage, gesso, chalk, gouache
and pencil. With palette knife and brush he captured the
very essence of the land (or 'the bones beneath the land' as
Ceri Richards once said) with a bravura and sensitivity that
came from a lifetime's involvement with it, sometimes paring

it down to an abstraction unhindered by detail but always managing to convey an emotional response that is rare in modern painting.

'As an emotional Celt,' he wrote in the catalogue of his exhibition at Heal's Mansard Gallery in 1974, 'I tend to paint from the heart; I enjoy the act of working the paint. My concern is to convey my emotions and enthusiasm for Wales through richness of texture, paint and colour; I see my work through music, song and poetry.' A retrospective exhibition of his work at the National Library of Wales in 2001 brought together an astonishing array of pictures done over 50 years in which he demonstrated just how magnificently he had achieved this aim.

Gwilym Prichard was born in 1931 in the Welsh-speaking village of Llanystumdwy, near Cricieth, where David Lloyd George had grown up and lies buried; his father was the local schoolmaster and church organist. 'I was brought up by the river Dwyfor,' he wrote, 'and spent most of my time fishing on the ever-changing flowing river. For me, nature and landscape were part of my life, the river my bloodstream.' After schooling at Porthmadog Grammar School, he did military service at Yatesbury in Wiltshire, where his training as a radar engineer was interrupted by a bout of rheumatic fever, after which, in 1950, he took a two-year course at the Normal College, Bangor, followed by a diploma course at Birmingham College of Art.

In 1954 he married Claudia Williams, an English painter trained at Chelsea School of Art who enjoyed a high reputation in her own right, and they settled in Llangefni on Anglesey where Prichard took up a post as a crafts teacher. The island became a major source of inspiration for him, especially the district between Pentraeth, Penmon and Beaumaris and taking in Priestholm (Puffin Island), the priory and lighthouse, a storm-beaten landscape in winter but alive with kaleidoscopic light the rest of the year. It was the silence, the windswept trees, the scudding clouds that appealed to him most, and he felt a strong sense of man's insignificance in the natural world – there are hardly any human figures in his work and if there are, they are almost lost in their surroundings.

Prichard came to prominence at a time when a sea change was getting under way in the public patronage of the visual arts in Wales: the Welsh Committee of the Arts Council, the National Eisteddfod, the Contemporary Arts Society and the Royal Cambrian Academy were beginning to take their responsibilities more seriously by offering commissions, exhibitions and prizes, and by trying to create a new audience for artists.

His first exhibition was at Porthmadog in 1952 and his first major award (a cheque for ten guineas) the Saxton Barton Memorial Prize in 1958. Soon he had found an appreciative public willing to buy his work, especially after he had begun exhibiting at the New Art Centre in Belgravia in 1958 and the Mansard Gallery at Heal's on Tottenham Court Road in 1966. He also had exhibitions at the Howard Roberts Gallery in Cardiff, the Tegfryn Gallery in Menai Bridge and the National Museum of Wales in Cardiff.

From 1966 to 1973 Prichard was Head of the Art Department at Friars School, Bangor. During a troubled year of teaching at Ratcliffe College in Leicester, where a new headmaster who cared nothing for the creative arts made life unpleasant by depriving him of the facilities he had been promised, he began to drink heavily and was now referred to the Drug and Alcohol In-patient Detoxification Unit in Southall, London; taken in hand by Max Glatt, and with the help of Alcoholics Anonymous, he never drank again.

Looking to make a fresh start, the family moved to Weobley in Herefordshire, renovating the vicarage at nearby Norton Canon, though both husband and wife continued to paint in north Wales. In 1979, unable to afford the upkeep of their old house, they moved back to Gwynedd, living first at Llanddona on Anglesey and then at Rhostryfan near Caernarfon, where Prichard taught occasionally in the Extra-Mural Department of the University College of North Wales, Bangor. Among his private patrons at this time were Lord Croft of Croft Castle near Leominster and Lady Mary Rennell of The Rodd, near Presteigne.

In 1984, now in their early 50s, the children having left home and in a bid to escape the damp climate of north Wales which was affecting Prichard's lungs, the couple set out in a shooting-brake across Europe, travelling through Italy, Greece and Provence, camping and painting along the way. On the leisurely homeward journey a year later, and equipped with only a school atlas, they found themselves by chance near Vannes on the Golfe de Morbihan on the southern coast of Brittany.

There they bought a former bakehouse in the centre of the medieval hill-town of Rochefort-en-Terre (population 700), some 40 miles to the north, where they lived as frugally as ever and gave art lessons to pay the bills. Prichard found in the Breton landscape the same qualities as he had liked in that of north-west Wales – stormy skies, sand-dunes, moorlands covered by heather and broom, and the gale-swept Atlantic of Finistère. He was, moreover, touched by the esteem in which he was held by local people and French art critics alike. The measure to which Prichard and Williams were admired by their French hosts is reflected in the fact that in 1995 they were each awarded the Silver Medal by the Academy of Arts, Sciences and Letters in Paris.

Their return to Wales in 1999 was to the Georgian town of Tenby in Pembrokeshire, where again Prichard found an enchanted landscape he could paint in colours – dusty pink, rich ochre, slate-blue – softer than those he had used in Snowdonia. The county with its glittering sea, sunny coastline and the gentler Preseli hills, land of the Mabinogion tales, provided him with an inner serenity reminiscent of what Gaugin briefly found at Pont-Aven in Brittany.

By the end of his career, Prichard's work was in most collections in Wales (except that of the National Museum which has long been negligent of indigenous artists) and had also been bought, outside Wales, by bodies as various as Lincoln College, Oxford, The Nuffield Foundation (Pictures for Hospitals), the Crédit Agricole bank, the French Embassy at Caracas, the Royal Artillery Regiment, British Steel, Marks & Spencer, Monsanto Chemicals and Southampton Art Gallery.

A shy but genial man, whose reserve and caution were complemented by the vivacity of his wife Claudia, Gwilym Prichard had the physical appearance of the Romantic artist: dark eyes, rugged complexion, shaggy black beard (which duly turned a patriarchal white), a large, spare frame and a deep voice in which he spoke the mellifluous Welsh of his native place. Of all the painters I have known, I have seldom come across one so contented with his lot, however hard his life had been. He never sought the limelight and only very reluctantly passed comment on the work of his contemporaries: he had spent his life doing what he wanted to do most and asked for no other reward.

Gwilym Arifor Prichard, painter: born Llanystumdwy, Caernarfonshire, 4 March 1931; married 1954 Claudia Williams (three sons, one daughter); died Tenby, 7 June 2015.

The Independent (29 June 2015)

OWEN ROBERTS

Pioneer of Welsh-language television

OWEN ROBERTS BELONGED to a stellar generation of news journalists who won their spurs at a critical moment for broadcasting in his native Wales. The BBC, for long having enjoyed a monopoly in news-gathering, suddenly found it had rivals in Television Wales and the West (TWW), and later Harlech Television (HTV). Both upstarts had begun training younger people and putting out programmes that competed for ratings previously considered the preserve of the BBC.

Roberts joined TWW as a graduate trainee director in 1961, having been recruited by the influential Wyn Roberts (now Lord Roberts of Conwy) who had spotted his potential as a hard-news man with a passion for current affairs, especially in Wales. He had just come down from Jesus College, Oxford, where he had read Modern History and played an active part in the affairs of the Dafydd ap Gwilym Society, that cradle of so many Welsh-speaking meritocrats who have gone on to make important contributions to the cultural life of their country. He delighted in speaking Welsh, his first language, in the Junior Common Room at Jesus and made many friends there. The boy from Niwbwrch in Anglesey, where his father was headmaster of the village school, matured into a sophisticated, cultured young patriot who was clearly going to make a name for himself.

Although he had appeared on radio several times since his schooldays at Llangefni Grammar School, he had a lot to learn about daily broadcasting schedules and the harsh realities of the commercial world. But he took to news gathering and, in due course, news management as to the manner born and soon had a reputation as a safe pair of hands in broadcasting circles.

The main news programme broadcast by the BBC at the time was *Heddiw* but it was not long before *Y Dydd* was challenging it in the quality of its journalism and its lively coverage of the whole of Wales. Roberts became the programme's editor in 1964 and, four years later, Head of News at HTV Wales.

His love of history remained a lifelong interest and left its mark on much of his work as a television producer. Among his most memorable early achievements was *The Just City*, a documentary dealing with the Welshmen who fought on the Republican side in the Spanish Civil War. The news, for him, was an early draft of history which demanded meticulous planning and editorial balance.

In 1972 he moved to BBC Wales as Head of News and Current Affairs and was later appointed Assistant Head of Programmes. The post was not without its pressures and tribulations, caused not least by the young militants of the Welsh Language Society. In the heated clashes between the broadcasting authorities and campaigners for a fourth channel broadcasting in Welsh, Roberts managed to keep his cool and displayed the gentle wit and bonhomie which endeared him to all. Even those who had raised a patrician eyebrow at the appointment of someone 'from the other side' were soon won over.

The delicate balance between provision of news programmes in the two languages of Wales was often at the heart of the broadcasters' thinking and policies. 'Those involved in Welsh-language programmes,' noted the BBC's Annual Report for 1972, 'see their world as their oyster.' Not so the English-language programme-makers of Wales, who – because significant events in English-speaking Wales were deemed to be the purview of the London media – were obliged to scratch for news in their own backyards. Mrs Jones's cow was a fabulous beast often drawn into the debate on both sides of the linguistic divide.

Most galling of all was that Owen Roberts, or Owen R as he was generally known to colleagues, to distinguish him from several others by the name of Owen, was from time to time called before the Broadcasting Council to listen to complaints that the output for which he was responsible was, in the words of the official historian of broadcasting in Wales, 'too preoccupied with traffic accidents, minor industrial disputes and other equally unscintillating matters'.

Roberts was still on a rising trajectory as a news manager when, in the mid-1970s, shortly after a car accident, he was diagnosed as having multiple sclerosis. He faced this adversity with exemplary courage and a dignified resolve which won the admiration of all who knew him.

In this he had the support and devotion of his wife, Ann Clwyd, since 1984 the Labour MP for the Cynon Valley and a well-known advocate of human rights for beleaguered minorities such as the Kurds. Her socialism chimed well with his own political views: she has described him as 'Welsh to the core and a socialist to the last', though he never went near anything to do with the Labour Party lest his editorial judgement be called into question. In his lifelong commitment to the social good, one of the hallmarks of his programme-making, Owen Roberts was passionate and articulate but never strident.

Owen Dryhurst Roberts, television executive with TWW, HTV and BBC Cymru/Wales: born Niwbwrch, Anglesey, 1 February 1939; married 1963 Ann Clwyd Lewis; died Cardiff, 23 October 2012.

The Independent (29 November 2012)

ARTHUR ROWLANDS

Policeman awarded the George Medal
after being blinded by assailant

ON THE NIGHT of 2 August 1961, at about three in the morning,
P.C. Arthur Rowlands was on patrol in the Machynlleth area
of Montgomeryshire when he saw a man acting suspiciously
in the vicinity of Pont-ar-Ddyfi just outside the town. There
had been a number of incidents involving summer visitors to
the area, and a spate of burglaries, and the police were on the
alert for any sign of wrongdoing.

When challenged, the man ran into some nearby buildings
but was cornered and confronted by the constable. 'You
shouldn't have come,' the man told him. 'I'm going to kill you.'
He then shot the policeman full in the face with a sawn-off
shotgun before running away across the fields. P.C. Rowlands
suffered severe injuries and was blinded for life.

Scotland Yard led the manhunt for Robert Boynton and
he was captured by local policemen ten days later with the
gun still in his possession. At his trial, he was found to be
criminally insane and sentenced to 32 years in Broadmoor,
where he died in 1994.

Rowlands was treated at hospitals in Chepstow, Cardiff
and Leamington, but surgeons failed to save his sight.
Remarkably, although with time, this sweet-natured man
bore no ill will towards the man who had maimed him,
recognizing that he was mad and therefore not responsible
for his actions. His Christian faith helped to sustain him
even as he lay in hospital in great pain and he was supported
by colleagues such as P.C. William Jones ('Will 82'), whom
he chose as his carer in hospital. Having joined the police
force in 1946, he never regretted his choice of career and

always encouraged young people to do the same. He and the three colleagues who arrested his assailant were awarded the George Medal.

But now, at the age of 39, his days as a policeman were over: he was facing an uncertain future in which he would have to remake his life. The father of two small children, he resolved to learn Braille so as not to forgo his pleasure in reading and with a view to finding useful employment.

He attended the College for the Blind in London, where he quickly learned to read again, and equipped himself for a voluntary job on the telephone switchboard at police headquarters in Caernarfon. His wife, Olive, went back to teaching.

Soon he had become a keen advocate of Guide Dogs for the Blind, working for the Gwynedd Guide Dogs Association. He helped to raise many thousands of pounds for the charity and took to visiting schools to show children what it means to be without sight. I once heard him describe how he remembered colours and places he had known before the dreadful incident on the Dyfi Bridge. When asked whether there was anything that irritated him he replied, with the sunny temperament that endeared him to many, that he wished people would not raise their voices when speaking to him just because he could not see them.

Determined to lead a full and active life, he did not let his blindness hinder his enjoyment of sport. He was often to be seen at the Farrar Road pitch, Bangor City's home ground. As a young man of 18 in 1940 he had had a trial for Manchester United and, with his grandson, who provided a commentary, he went to Edinburgh in 2007 when Wales played Scotland at rugby. He continued to walk the lower slopes of Snowdon, even going to the summit several times with his son. 'At least I didn't have to worry about the mist,' he remarked wryly. He was also a regular contributor to Welsh programmes on Radio Cymru. The last time I heard him he was speaking about the case of P.C. David Rathband, the policeman blinded by gunman Raoul Moat in July 2010, who was found dead at his home in Northumberland in February 2012.

A fluent Welsh-speaker, born in Bala, Meirionnydd, and brought up as a farmer's son in nearby villages, Rowlands was a man of broad culture and a dry wit. In 1981 he was admitted to the Gorsedd of Bards, taking the White Robe, and in the year following he was given an honorary MA by the University of Wales. A full account of his life is given in Enid Wyn Baines's, *Mae'r Dall yn Gweld* (1983). In his book *Murder Was My Business* (1971), the former Assistant Detective Commissioner John du Rose described Rowlands as the bravest man he had ever known.

Arthur Rees Rowlands, police constable and promoter of Guide Dogs for the Blind: born Bala, Meirionnydd, 14 May 1922; married 1949 Olive Jones (deceased 2005; one son, one daughter); died Caernarfon, Gwynedd, 2 December 2012.

The Independent (28 January 2013)

JOHN ROWLANDS

Novelist who explored the darker side of the human mind

AMONG THE PROSE-WRITERS who began making names for themselves in the 1960s, when the novel was enjoying a new vogue in Wales, John Rowlands was unusual in that, far from trying to appeal to popular taste, he ploughed a lone furrow as an author for whom the exploration of the inner life and its complexities was far more important. The consequences were that his seven novels, though admired by his peers, were thought 'difficult' and 'highbrow' by those who wanted merely a good yarn or an easy read. They were not the kind of 'stuff' that the proselytising Librarian of Cardiganshire, Alun R. Edwards, wanted for his shelves because ordinary borrowers turned up their noses at anything they thought 'arty' or 'highfalutin'.

John Rowlands was from an early age a writer for whom the life of the mind meant a great deal. Born and brought up on a small farm near Trawsfynydd in Meirionnydd, he was encouraged by his parents to read and discuss literature, and to take every opportunity of competing at local eisteddfodau. His mother was a fine memoirist and his older sister Catrin, who was also to become a novelist, was already writing competent prose, and for that reason he tried his hand at verse. But the language of the county school at Blaenau Ffestiniog, where he was a contemporary of the poet Gwyn Thomas and the novelist Eigra Lewis Roberts, was English and, coming from a wholly Welsh-speaking home and district, he made little headway. Instead, he turned to music; playing the piano was to remain a passion for the rest of his life and in all his novels the role of music is paramount.

It was while an undergraduate at the University College

of North Wales, Bangor, where he took first-class Honours in Welsh, that John Rowlands became a writer. There he fell under the spell of John Gwilym Jones, playwright and critic, who nurtured in him the talent that was to blossom almost immediately. His first novel, *Lle bo'r Gwenyn* (1960), was written in Bangor, as was his second, *Yn Ôl i'w Teyrnasoedd* (1963). Both these books reflect their author's fascination with human psychology and a bleak contemporary world in which the individual is often seen as isolated, introspective and vulnerable.

His next novel, *Ienctid yw 'Mhechod* (1965), caused a fluttering in the dovecotes of literary Wales, but for the wrong reason. His publisher, Emlyn Evans, had steadfastly refused to publish it on the grounds that it contained explicit descriptions of sex between a minister and a member of his congregation, only to find on his return from holiday that the owner of the press, the bullish Alun Talfan Davies, had ordered the book to be printed, whereupon Evans resigned. The passages that offended Evans are, by today's standards, only mildly lubricious but in 1965 they caused as much stir in Wales as had *Lady Chatterley's Lover* in England five years before. When an English version, *A Taste of Apples*, appeared in 1966 hardly a hair was turned. Sex remained a central concern for Rowlands in all his subsequent work.

From Bangor Rowlands went to do doctoral research on the poetry of Dafydd ap Gwilym at Jesus College, Oxford, by which time he knew himself to be a novelist who would explore the human mind in all its aspects. 'The mind is wide,' says one of his characters, 'as wide as the material universe or wider. It's a man's duty to think and discover a purpose to all things, especially his own life.' While at Trinity College, Carmarthen, where he was lecturing in 1968, he wrote *Llawer Is na'r Angylion*, in which the chief character yearns for personal freedom from the suffocating traditions of rural Wales, particularly chapel hypocrisy and village gossip. In his next novel, too, *Bydded Tywyllwch* (1969), the heroine who escapes to a life of promiscuity in London asks, 'What is normal?' The pleasure of reading these books is almost wholly cerebral and many readers were put off by the dark world they explored.

An even more complex theme is expertly handled in *Arch ym Mhrâg* (1972), which is about the political aspirations of young people in the Czechoslovakia of 1968. Rowlands, by now a lecturer at St David's University College, Lampeter, happened to be in the country at the time of the Soviet invasion in 1968 and returned, with the help of a Welsh Arts Council travel-grant, in the summer of 1971. Once again it is not the external events or ideologies of 'the Prague Spring' that are of primary importance in this novel but 'the interior landscape' of the protagonists' minds. Least convincing of all is when the author brings his main character to Wales to make common cause with language campaigners of the late 1960s. 'We are struggling,' says one, 'to tighten the rope which binds us to the past. We must be fools.'

Rowlands moved to a lectureship in the Welsh Department at the University College of Wales, Aberystwyth, in 1975. His seventh novel, *Tician Tician* (1978), was once more set in Academe but, no campus romp, it explored the crisis faced by the Welsh language even in one of its last bastions, in particular the effect the prospect of its imminent demise has on the mind of a young lecturer who is almost certainly meant to be Rowlands himself. A very shy man who would blush profusely when addressed in conversation and was rarely to be seen on social occasions, he nevertheless felt the threat to his language very acutely and was stout in his defence of students who broke the law in a bid to secure a degree of legal status for it. There was nothing comforting or uplifting about his novels: they were meant to disturb our complacency and to challenge our intellect.

His academic work was of the first water. In the volume

Dafydd ap Gwilym a Chanu Serch yr Oesoedd Canol (1975), which he edited, he re-examined the topic of his doctoral research. The symposium *Sglefrio ar Eiriau* (1992) brought together eight of the leading critics in Wales to discuss, in the light of recent literary theory but shorn of dogma and the worst jargon, various aspects of contemporary Welsh literature. The same could be said of *Y Sêr yn eu Graddau* (2000) which dealt with the modern Welsh novel. The last-named appeared in the series *Y Meddwl a'r Dychymyg Cymreig*, edited by Rowlands, which includes some of the most advanced writing to appear in Welsh in recent times. He was awarded a personal Chair at Aberystwyth in 1996 and, after his retirement in 2003, was made Emeritus.

Rowlands made only two excursions into English. He contributed an elegant monograph on the popular novelist T. Rowland Hughes (1903–49) to the *Writers of Wales* series (1975) which opens, not entirely with tongue in cheek, 'Let us admit at the outset that there is no such thing as The Welsh Novel.' With Glyn Jones, he wrote a visitor's guide to writing in twentieth-century Wales, *Profiles* (1980), from which, characteristically, he excluded any mention of himself; it was left to his co-author to ensure that a note about him appeared on the book's back flap. He also translated (with R. Bryn Williams) Lorca's play *Bodas de sangre* as *Priodas Gwaed* (1977) and wrote a study of Saunders Lewis as literary critic in the *Llên y Llenor* series (1990).

He co-edited *Taliesin,* the magazine of the Welsh Academy, from 1993 to 1998, and wrote a regular food column for the monthly journal *Barn* in which he rated restaurants in Wales and the Border counties, often garnishing his reports with literary references. For a few years he and his wife turned their home near Groeslon, Gwynedd, into a restaurant, at which he would serve at table; the place was called Y Goeden Eirin in tribute to John Gwilym Jones, author of a celebrated collection of short stories with that title, who had put him on the road to becoming a writer.

John Rowlands, novelist: born Trawsfynydd, Meirionnydd, 14 August 1938; married Eluned (one daughter, two sons); died 23 February 2015.

The Independent (17 May 2015)

STAN STENNETT

Welsh comedian who excelled in pantomime

THE VETERAN COMIC entertainer Stan Stennett's 70-year career as a musician and actor began with *Workers' Playtime* in the post-war period and ended with bit-parts in television shows as late as 2008. After serving with the Royal Artillery, he began as a jazz trumpeter and guitarist with the Harmoniacs, playing with the Joe Loss and Ted Heath bands, and was resident comedian on *Welsh Rarebit* and *The Black and White Minstrel Show*, but soon found he also had talent as a comedian.

His first appearances in this mode were with Max Miller in the late 1940s. Over the next two decades he worked with most of the famous names of British and American showbiz, including Billy Daniels, Johnnie Ray, Chico Marx, James Cagney, Morecambe and Wise, Ken Dodd, Ronnie Corbett, and Jon Pertwee. This was a boom time for variety shows as the rigours of the war gave way to comparative affluence and a more relaxed attitude to popular entertainment, and he was rarely out of work thereafter.

By 1970 he had appeared with the Minstrels seven times, helping to win the Golden Rose award at the Montreux Festival, and had worked with comedians such as George Chisholm and Leslie Crowther. It was thus he learned his craft as a stage comedian with a talent for playing the fool, in particular for making children laugh. His first appearance in pantomime was at the Grand Theatre, Swansea, in a performance of *Little Red Riding Hood*. With a humour that was broad, warm and clean, he went through the traditional routines of which children never tire, and his singalongs and rhyming ditties brought smiles to the faces of their parents and teachers as well. One of his most popular acts was as Billy and Bonzo, in which he played both the gormless Billy and his rascal pooch Bonzo. By this simple device he was able to make comedy that was spellbinding, surreal and sometimes moving. He held the record of having appeared in pantomime for five consecutive years at Cardiff's New Theatre.

Stan Stennett was born on a farm near Bridgend in 1925 and brought up by his grandmother in Gorseinon, near Swansea, and Cardiff; born out of wedlock, he was never told who his father was. He left school at 15 and worked as a delivery boy with Pickfords before being called up into the Royal Artillery; he was sent to Normandy shortly after the D-Day landings.

His ambition to work on the stage was first fired by listening to radio programmes on the Welsh Home Service, particularly shows like Mai Jones's *Welsh Rarebit*. Like so many of his generation, he was shaped by the war and its aftermath and always took the view that the pictures were much better on the wireless. His one-man show *Bless 'Em All*, a compendium of wartime nostalgia, was a huge success among those who could remember the Blitz, the blackout and rationing.

But it was television that gave him his break as an actor. He appeared in *Coronation Street* in 1960 and in several broadcasts of *Play for Today*. This work continued for the next 40 years: he played Sid Hooper in *Crossroads* from 1982 to 1987, Cyril Fuller in *Heartbeat* in 1999 and Wally Brindle in *Casualty* in 2002. His part as an American GI on the run from the military police who holds up Tish Hope at her cottage in *Crossroads* was among the more gripping episodes of that soap opera and showed him capable of playing more serious parts than he had hitherto been given. Unfortunately, the gunman was sentenced to 20 years in gaol and so he never appeared again. Stennett made a return to *Coronation Street* in 1976 as Hilda Ogden's brother Norman Crabtree.

At various times in his career Stan Stennett managed theatres in Tewkesbury, Hereford, Caerffili and Porthcawl. In 1984 he was at the Roses Theatre in Tewkesbury where he interviewed his friend Eric Morecambe about his career. The idea was to get Morecambe to sit quietly on stage at the end of the show but instead he rushed about pretending to play all the instruments in the band, after which he suffered his third heart attack and collapsed in the wings as the curtain came down, dying later in hospital.

His hobby was aviation: he held a private pilot's licence and was named Flyer of the Year by the Royal Aeronautical Club in 1955. He was the subject of *This Is Your Life* and in 1979 was awarded the MBE for his services to the entertainment industry and his patronage of many charities in south Wales. He was particularly proud of his association with the Grand Order of Water Rats and with the Cardiff College of Music and Drama, where he was given a Fellowship. Despite the loss of his vast collection of memorabilia in a house-fire in 1999, he published his autobiography, *Fully Booked*, in 2010 in collaboration with Terry Grandin.

The last time I saw him was in a queue at a chip shop in north Cardiff where, extrovert as ever before an audience, however small, he was making customers grin at his wisecracks. 'Did you hear about the cowboy who walked into a car saleroom in Germany and said, 'Audi!"

Stanley Llewellyn Stennett (Stan Stennett), comedian: born Bridgend, Glamorgan, 30 July 1925, Cardiff; married 1948 Betty (two sons); died Cardiff, 26 November 2013.

The Independent (28 November 2013)

GWYN THOMAS

Poet who combined scholarship with a playful technique

THE POET AND scholar Gwyn Thomas was one of the most prolific Welsh writers of his generation and, despite his erudition and the complexity of his work, one of the most genuinely popular. Not for nothing was he appointed National Poet of Wales in 2006, only the second to hold that prestigious post.

Outstanding among his contemporaries in his readiness to use the broken constructions and halting, often anglicized vocabulary of modern colloquial Welsh, he was able to make his verse accessible to a wide readership, including younger readers who responded to the playful way in which he subverted traditional meanings and made poetry a medium for fun. His early work, in particular, was joyful, witty and sometimes hilarious, reflecting a young man's delight at the quiddities of life, especially a child's idiosyncratic grasp of language: the title of his fourth collection, *Enw'r Gair* (1972), was suggested by his small son's asking, as he learnt to talk, 'What's the name of the word?'

He wrote poems in a register which, however much it shared the traditional functions of Welsh poetry, disconcerted some critics who complained that his work was too close to doggerel on account of its highly colloquial, seemingly slapdash rhythms and rhymes. It is more to the point that, while he took risks and courted banality, sentimentality and a certain diffuseness, he opened up new areas of human experience which would have been closed, or at least distorted, by a loftier or more polished technique. His use of rhyme, in particular, was deft, often startling and sometimes downright comic as in the manner of Ogden Nash, but the reader was never allowed to forget his serious intent. He was able to speak of Hiroshima, Belsen, apartheid, the war in Iraq, and the Third World without sounding in the least portentous or phoney.

His most important scholarly work was undoubtedly *Y Bardd Cwsg a'i Gefndir* (1971), a major study of Ellis Wynne (1671–1734), Churchman, Tory, Royalist and author of a prose masterpiece translated as *Visions of the Sleeping Bard* which was based on the work of Roger L'Estrange and the Spanish writer Quevedo, and he contributed a monograph on Wynne to the *Writers of Wales* series (1984). A selection of his essays on other literary topics, including the poets Siôn Cent and R. Williams Parry, appeared as *Gair am Air* in 2000.

But he was also concerned to make the ancient poetry and prose tradition of Wales more easily available to the modern reader. In *Yr Aelwyd Hon* (1970), which he published in association with his colleagues Bedwyr Lewis Jones and Derec Llwyd Morgan, he presented a selection of the earliest Welsh poetry in modern Welsh versions, beginning with the *Cynfeirdd*, notably the sixth-century Aneirin and Taliesin, who wrote in Old Welsh in 'the Old North' – what are now southern Scotland, Cumbria and much of Lancashire and Yorkshire. It was followed by *Y Traddodiad Barddol* (1976), a critical survey which takes the story through the golden age of Dafydd ap Gwilym in the fourteenth century to the Poets of the Gentry who came into their own after the loss of Welsh independence in 1282 and flourished for another 300 years or so. He was also in favour of exegesis in English of the work of more recent Welsh writers, co-editing the volume *Presenting Saunders Lewis* in 1973, the first study of the many-faceted Lewis in a language which he had wanted to see driven from the land of Wales.

Out of his desire to help Welsh literature reach new readers, Gwyn Thomas also undertook the work of translation: with Kevin Crossley-Holland he translated editions for children of *The Mabinogion* (1984), *The Quest for Olwen* (1988) and *The Tale of Taliesin* (1992), while his modern Welsh version of the medieval legend *Culhwch ac Olwen* (1988) won the Tir na n-Og Prize for children's literature in the year of its publication. The rich idioms and his command of the natural rhythms of Welsh, his native language, made these books classics of their genre and were widely admired.

Gwyn Thomas was born in 1936 at Tanygrisiau and brought up in nearby Blaenau Ffestiniog, in the heart of the slate-quarrying districts of Meirionnydd; his father was not a quarryman, as were most men in the town, but a baker. Educated at the University College of North Wales, Bangor, and Jesus College, Oxford, where he was awarded his doctorate and took a full part in the affairs of the Dafydd ap Gwilym Society, he taught for a year at his old school before being appointed lecturer in the Welsh Department at Bangor in 1961. He was given a personal Chair in 1980, becoming Head of Department in 1992, and he was to remain in Bangor until his retirement. His autobiography, *Llyfr Gwyn*, appeared in 2015.

Besides *Enw'r Gair*, he published 16 volumes of poetry, beginning with *Chwerwder yn y Ffynhonnau* (1962), *Y Weledigaeth Haearn* (1965) and *Ysgyrion Gwaed* (1968), which contains his splendid radio ode, '*Blaenau*'. These early poems were not juvenilia but mature responses to the complexity of the modern world, finely crafted, carrying a strong emotional current, contemporary in their themes but harnessing images from the Welsh past to convey a sense of profundity and irony which is most effective.

The concern for communication and contemporaneity which informed his scholarly work was central to Gwyn Thomas's creative activity, which had nothing of the ivory tower about it: he caught the mood of the Swinging Sixties, with their new technology, in the line '*Mae'r tempo wedi newid, nid oes dim yr un fath*' ('The tempo has changed, nothing is the same any more'). He had been a keen cinemagoer since his schooldays and wrote for both radio and television, and in *Cadwynau yn y Meddwl* (1976) paid tribute to Martin Luther King in a long poem written specifically for the small screen. Indeed, he went so far as to coin a new word, *llunyddiaeth*, meaning 'visual writing', which he argued should take its place with *llenyddiaeth*, the traditional word for 'literature'. In 1993 he translated and adapted Shakespeare for the joint S4C/BBC series *Animated Shakespeare*.

More poetry flowed from him at a rate faster than any other Welsh poet, including the Stakhanovite Bobi Jones: *Y Pethau Diwethaf a Phethau Eraill* (1975), *Croesi Traeth* (1978), *Symud y Lliwiau* (1981), *Wmgawa* (an attempt to convey the cry of Johnny Weissmuller as Tarzan, 1984), *Am Ryw Hyd* (1986), *Darllen y Meini* (1998), *Gwelaf Afon* (1990), *Apocalups Yfory* (2005), and *Teyrnas y Tywyllwch* (2007), all added a cubit to his stature as one of the most inventive poets of his generation. These books are more contemplative than the earlier work and reflect not only his own awareness of the passing of the years but of 'the blood-soaked century' in which he had lived. The last-named book took as its theme the horrors of the concentration-camps and owed something to Martin Gilbert's *The Holocaust*.

A selection of his early poems in his own English translations, together with others by Joseph P. Clancy, was published in Amsterdam in 1982 under the title *Living a Life* and a selection of his poems written between 1962 and 1986 appeared as *Gweddnewidio* in 2000. He gave a typically genial account of his early life in *Bywyd Bach* (2006) and produced, with the photographer Jeremy Moore, a tribute to his hometown in the coffee-table book *Blaenau Ffestiniog* (2007) in which the town's flinty topography is seen through a native's affectionate eye.

Side by side with this extraordinary output, Thomas published a Welsh translation of Beckett's *Fin de partie* and Peter Weiss's *Trotzki im Exil*. Then, just to remind his youngest readers that reading can be fun, he brought out *Sawl Math o Gath* (2002), in the manner of Old Possum, for which he composed his own spoof puffs, including one attributed to Aristotle to the effect that reading the book had been a '*cathartig*' experience for him.

As National Poet, a role he filled with relish, he wrote a number of poems about public events, always seeking evidence that, despite the horrors of the modern world, humankind is capable of better things. One of the first he wrote in this capacity was in praise of a schoolgirl whose kidney, after she had been killed by a horse, had saved the life of another young woman, a positive act which he contrasted with the London bombings of July 2005. The respective functions of the National Poet of Wales and the English Poet Laureate were never so clearly demonstrated as when Gwyn Thomas and Andrew Motion spoke at the Millennium Centre in Cardiff in April 2007.

Gwyn Thomas, poet and scholar: born Tanygrisiau, Meirionnydd, 2 September 1936; Lecturer in Welsh, University College of North Wales, Bangor, 1961–80, Professor of Welsh, 1980–2001, and Emeritus; National Poet of Wales, 2006–7; married 1964 Jennifer Roberts (two sons, one daughter); died 14 April 2016.

JON MANCHIP WHITE

Prolific American writer who was born in Cardiff

JON MANCHIP WHITE was primarily a narrator of extraordinary events which take place in exotic settings. Most of his novels, some 20 in all, have to do with a race, or an escape, or a test of endurance, skill or moral fibre. Not strong on characterization, he was an adroit raconteur and liked gripping yarns that do not so much unfold as gallop along, sometimes breathtakingly, so that the reader is immediately immersed in the action and caught up in a spiralling parabola of excitement.

As a novelist he had a penchant for people who are in some way past their prime and there is more than a touch of Hemingway in his preoccupation with physical ordeals and the minutiae of military training, the weaponry and equipment of his protagonists, often soldiers and sportsmen. Among other novelists whose work he admired were Rex Warner, Julien Gracq and Julien Green, and among painters, Chirico, Ernst and Masson, where the dream-image is sharp and bright.

His first novel, *Mask of Dust* (1953), published in the USA as *The Last Race*, is about the world of the international motor Grand Prix. It is set in northern Italy, where the crowd regard this spectacular and lethal sport as the modern equivalent of charioteering. The hero is a British driver who has been a fighter pilot during the war and is now attempting to prove he has not lost his nerve and expertise at the wheel so that he might retain the favours of his young and beautiful wife.

Another of White's favourite themes is the reward or punishment of anti-social behaviour. In three of his novels the main character is on the run from conventional society: in *No Home But Heaven* (1957) a gypsy is in conflict with the Welfare State; *The Mercenaries* (1958) is an escape drama set in Argentina after the fall of Perón; *Hour of the Rat* (1962) deals with the trial of a British civil servant who has killed a member of a Japanese delegation, his former persecutor in a prisoner of war camp.

An exception to these tales of derring-do is *The Rose in the Brandy Glass* (1965) which relates how a retired cavalry colonel quixotically refuses to sign an inaccurate statement so that he might share in an inheritance. It is White's most ambitious attempt to write a novel in which the mainspring is social and psychological conflict rather than mere adventure, though it exposes his limitations in the delineation of character.

White defended himself against his critics by lamenting the decline of the novel in Britain and the taste for large themes and broad canvases. 'The solid, educated, extensive, cultural, book-buying class with its knowledge of and interest in the great world to whom the British novelist once addressed himself has vanished,' he wrote in 1972. 'The novelist is now uncertain of the nature and character of his reader. Since they celebrate the qualities of energy and ambition, novels of my kind are not popular in Britain. When British life has regained some of its native vigour and breadth, the characters and situations that novelists like me write about will be more in fashion.'

Jon Manchip White was born in Cardiff in 1924. His comfortable home was in Cathedral Road, one of the city's grandest avenues, and a few doors from where Joseph Conrad finished writing *The Nigger of the 'Narcissus'*. He was of seafaring stock – sailors and shipowners who had plied their trades in the Bristol Channel for centuries. Among his ancestors was Rawlins White, a poor, illiterate fisherman who, rather than renounce his Protestant faith, was burned at the stake during the Marian persecution of 1555. On a visit to his native city in 1990, the novelist paid filial tribute at the bronze plaque commemorating the martyr that is now on a wall of the gents' department of a major store. His book *Rawlins White: Patriot to Heaven* appeared in 2011. His father was the only member of his family not to go to sea, though he made a living as part-owner and managing director of the Taff Vale Shipping Company. At the time of the boy's birth, the economic slump was having a severe effect on the shipping industry and his father struggled to keep his business from bankruptcy. In 1932 he contracted tuberculosis and, to lessen the risk of infection, his son was sent to a boarding school in north London, where he received a first-rate education. During school holidays he was employed by the *Western Mail* with the rather grand title of Our Theatre Correspondent, which gave him a taste for seeing his name in print.

During his time at school White decided the best way to reverse the decline of his family's fortunes was to win a scholarship to university. This he did, entering St Catherine's College, Cambridge, with an Open Exhibition in English in 1942. In the year following he came of age for military conscription and joined the Naval Training Unit. During the war he served on naval convoys ferrying troops and materials across the Atlantic and, as hostilities drew to a close, was transferred to the Welsh Guards. He met his wife, Valerie, a nurse, during the celebrations in London on VE Day. In 1947 he resumed his studies at Cambridge and took a degree in English, Prehistoric Archaeology and Oriental Languages. Shortly afterwards he was given a job with the Keeper of the Egyptian and Assyrian Department at the British Museum.

He published extensively in the fields of Anthropology and Egyptology, including a translation of Samivel's *The Glory of Egypt* (1956) and *Everyday Life in Ancient Egypt* (1964), and edited a number of important texts such as Harold Carter's *The Tomb of Tutankhamun* (1972) and J.H.

Breasted's *A History of the Ancient Egyptians* (1991). He also edited Norman Douglas's *Introduction to Old Calabria* (1993) and introduced an edition of Robert Louis Stevenson's *Travels with a Donkey in the Cevennes* (1996).

By 1956 he knew he wanted to be a writer. He had already published two slim volumes of verse with the Fortune Press and another, *The Rout of San Romano* (1952), with Hand and Flower Press, but now wanted more experience that could go to the making of novels. He had joined the newly established BBC Television Service as a story-editor, where he not only read hundreds of scripts but also began writing original dramas. In 1960 he left his post as Senior Executive Officer in the Foreign Service in order to live as a full-time writer. He found work with Samuel Bronston Productions in Paris and Madrid, all the while travelling in Europe and southern Africa.

Among his books published during the 1960s were *Marshal of France: The Life and Times of Maurice, Comte de Saxe* (1962), the natural son of Augustus II, Elector of Saxony, who won the battle of Fontenoy in 1745 and from whom the novelist George Sand was descended, and the study *Diego Velázques, Painter and Courtier* (1969). His travels in South-West Africa bore fruit in *The Land God Made in Anger* (1969). A more substantial collection of his poems appeared from Chatto & Windus as *The Mountain Lion* in 1971.

In 1965 he felt a need to change direction again and, ever the wanderer, moved to the United States, a place which had engaged his sympathies since his time in Cambridge, during which he had written a dissertation on the Pueblo Indians. At the suggestion of the distinguished critic Cleanth Brook, whom he had met at the American Embassy in London, he applied for a post as writer-in-residence at the University of Texas at El Paso and was appointed in 1967. Ten years later he moved to Knoxville where he became Lindsay Young Professor of English, a post in which he remained until his retirement. He enjoyed the special status afforded to creative writers on most campuses in the USA and became an American citizen in the 1970s.

Two novels of this period are perhaps among his best: *Nightclimber* (1968) and *The Game of Troy* (1971), both of which were reissued in *Fevers and Chills: Three Extravagant Tales* in 1983. In the first the hero is an art historian who is prey to the habit, said to be much in vogue in pre-war Cambridge, of climbing high and dangerous buildings, and whose obsession is exploited by a millionaire collector in search of mysterious Greek treasure. In the image of the nightclimber White hit on a symbol for the force that drives many of his characters and inspires the kind of adventure he excelled in recounting. They are impelled to push their luck, to take more than a calculated risk, constantly in danger of falling disastrously to earth.

In *The Game of Troy* a strain of phantasmagoria appeared in his writing. The plot is based on the legend of the Minotaur. The central character, an architect, is commissioned by a Texas millionaire, with whose wife he has fallen in love, to make a labyrinth, complete with elaborate lighting and air-conditioning. He finds himself being pursued by the murderous husband along the winding corridors of this nightmarish maze as the story reaches its bloody climax.

White's academic career at El Paso gave him ample opportunity to explore the American Southwest and Mexico. He wrote *Cortés and the Downfall of the Aztec Empire* (1971), *A World Elsewhere: One Man's Fascination with the American Southwest* (1975) and *Everyday Life of the North American Indians* (1979). His right-of-centre political views – he always sneered at 'socialists and crypto-socialists' and was especially caustic about readers of the *New Statesman* – were expressed in *What to Do When the Russians Come: a Survivor's Handbook* (1984), an hysterical tract warning that the Soviet Union was about to engulf the world, which he wrote in collaboration with Robert Conquest; the book's rather puzzling advice is to run away and settle in a free country.

Although he kept in touch with friends in Wales, notably Alun Hoddinott, the composer for whose music he wrote words, White was not remembered in the land of his birth. When my *Oxford Companion to the Literature of Wales* appeared in 1986, he wrote me a tart letter complaining he had been omitted and I had to confess that I had never thought of him as a Welshman, though after re-reading some of his books I made sure an entry appeared in the second edition that came out in 1998.

At the time of his brief visit to Cardiff in 1990, the first in 20 years, White was writing a memoir which appeared as *The Journeying Boy: Scenes from a Welsh Childhood*, in 1991. The book is an attempt to lay the ghosts of his past, particularly his father's consumption, and takes the form of an expatriate's fond memories of a city and its docklands which had changed so much that he barely recognized them.

Jon Manchip White, writer: born Cardiff, 23 June 1924; Professor of English, University of Texas at El Paso, 1967–77; Lindsay Young Professor of English, University of Tennessee, 1977–86 and Associate; married 1946 Valerie Leighton (deceased, two daughters); died 30 July 2013.

The Independent (16 September 2013)

JOHN WRIGHT

Painter who climbed mountains and made film

JOHN WRIGHT, FORMER Principal of Newport Art College, knew from the age of five that he wanted to become an artist. A schoolmate showed him how to draw an Arab and, after realising he too could replicate the image with a few deft lines, he drew it on every available surface. His pleasure knew no bounds and the epiphany remained with him for the rest of his life.

He was born in Catford, London, in 1931, one of a fireman's three sons. Sent to Wales as an evacuee in 1940, he took to the people and countryside of Carmarthenshire with such affection that by the time he entered Carmarthen School of Art, he considered himself to be Welsh and would be closely associated with the arts scene in Wales as painter, film-maker, animateur and designer. He was fortunate in having been put into the care of a man who owned an antiques business known as The Old Curiosity Shop and whose brother owned a second-hand bookshop. These were perfect places for the young aesthete to spend much of his free time. He was also deeply affected by the scenery of west Wales, with which he became acquainted on Sunday outings with Uncle Reg and Uncle Will, and the coves around Mwnt and the farms of the Cothi valley became his first subjects.

While still a student, he saw a film called *High Conquest*, the story based on Edward Whymper and the climbing of the Matterhorn. The sight of the moonlit peak from the main street of Zermatt a few years later left an indelible impression on him. He now set out to climb every ridge of the Matterhorn over 4,000 metres and soon became a seasoned alpinist. Many of his paintings depict mountain scenery, sometimes distorted as if reflected in a mirror but always vibrant and majestic. He became a member of the Alpine Club, often climbing without a guide on mountains where many have lost their lives.

At about the same time he discovered a passion for bullfighting, after reading Hemingway's *Death in the Afternoon*, a novel that taught him to think for himself. He became an aficionado of the bullring and on 28 July 1965 saw one of the most memorable *corridas* of recent times when Antonio Ordóñez and Paco Camino, two of Spain's greatest matadors, appeared 'in an afternoon of overwhelming triumph'. In an essay he contributed to my symposium, *Artists in Wales* (1971), he wrote, 'No European artists have moved me more than Ordóñez and Camino.' Slim and lithe of body in a matador's mould, and a natty dresser, he was a man whom many women found attractive. He also had a relationship with alcohol and could be very good company late at night.

Another discovery was that he could write, a talent nurtured by Keidrych Rhys, who ran the Druid Press and published the magazine *Wales* in Carmarthen's Lammas Street, where he was taken on as an assistant. Browsing among the famously untidy shelves, it was here he read Dylan Thomas and R.S. Thomas for the first time; both poets became inspirations for the mature artist. He also wrote short stories, one of which appeared in the Faber anthology *Welsh Short Stories* (1956) edited by George Ewart Evans in 1959. But it was as a painter that he concentrated his energies. Even so, he once told me that he thought of himself as a literary painter and wanted his pictures to tell a story first and foremost. In 1953 he exhibited at the first of the Arts Council's open exhibitions in Cardiff and thereafter his pictures could be seen in many of the major galleries of Wales, England and America.

He won the Llandaff Festival Prize in 1961. In 1968 he was presented with a Medal by the municipality of Arles for a documentary film and, in the year following with the Montera d'Or, the highest award at the Montpellier Film Festival. Thus began a love affair with the landscapes and cultures of the Mediterranean. As a member of the '56 Group he was part of a campaign for modernist art against those who were content with more traditional scenes. He was a designer for the publisher Chatto and Windus. Among the public bodies to which he was appointed were the Council for Industrial Design and the Welsh Arts Council.

In 1965 he joined the Newport College of Art and Design, where he had a number of distinguished colleagues such as Tom Rathmell, Ernest Zobole, John Selway, Jeffrey Steele and Anthony Stevens. The college also produced budding film-makers and graphic designers, rare birds in the Wales of the 1960s. Op Art, a system of pure abstraction that relied on mathematical progressions and the theories of the psychology of perception, was the order of the day.

John Wright, the least autocratic of principals, and one of the youngest, allowed his staff the freedom to develop their own interests. The Film Department at Newport was the only one of its kind in Wales but under the direction of Harley Jones, sometime assistant to the documentary-maker John Grierson, it allowed students to express themselves in a modernist idiom. But Wright's career as principal of a small but progressive college was to be cut short: he resigned from his post in 1986, and disappeared from public view for many years thereafter. Very few of his former colleagues knew what had become of him or where he was. He had turned his back on Britain, which he called 'Nightmare Island', and died in his beloved Spain.

John Edward Wright, painter and designer, Principal of Newport Art College, Monmouthshire: born Catford, London, 26 May 1931; married first Lindy Ellis, second Muriel Baines, third 1987 Elizabeth Berry; died Estepona, Andalusia, 9 July 2013.

The Independent (6 October 2013)

Meic Stephens

Welsh*lives*
Gone but not forgotten

75 obituaries of eminent people

y Lolfa

MEIC STEPHENS
My Shoulder to the Wheel

AN AUTOBIOGRAPHY

£9.95

More Welsh Lives is just one of a whole
range of publications from Y Lolfa. For a full
list of books currently in print, send now
for your free copy of our new full-colour
catalogue. Or simply surf into our website

www.ylolfa.com

for secure on-line ordering.

TALYBONT CEREDIGION CYMRU SY24 5HE
e-mail ylolfa@ylolfa.com
website www.ylolfa.com
phone (01970) 832 304
fax 832 782

Ask for a print quote!
01970 832 304